Reincarnation in a Nutshell

Why Reincarnation Is Real

Else Byskov and Maria McMahon

Authors: Else Byskov, M.A., B.A. and Maria McMahon, BSc, Dip. H.E.Hyp/NLP/BSc

Cover Design: Sharon Brownlie

All images used with permission or under license

Copyright© 2019 by Else Byskov and Maria McMahon

Foreword:

Welcome to the first book in the Nutshell series....

In this series we are going to explain various topics of a spiritual nature – topics that have been puzzling humankind since the dawn of time. Among the topics there will be: the question of life after death, reincarnation, fate and the law of karma, what or who is the Earth, is there a God, what is the structure of life, human evolution and many more.

It is logical that when we move into the spiritual realm, we have to have access to insight about this realm. We have this insight from Martinus, the Danish visionary and mystic, who lived from 1890 to 1981. When he was 30, Martinus experienced an expansion of his consciousness which enabled him to see beyond the physical level and into the spiritual level, where everything has its origin. Martinus had achieved cosmic consciousness, and he had access to the sea of knowledge that the Universe holds. When Martinus died at the age of 90, he left a legacy of 10.000 pages of spiritual wisdom and his work is the most complete spiritual revelation ever disclosed to humankind. There is nothing like it. There is nothing even close to it in scope, depth and outlook. It is a completely unique work and it answers all the big questions and then some. It is an inexhaustible source of insight about both the physical and the spiritual levels of existence. We can also say that it is a comprehensive philosophy of life, death and the mystery of both. The Martinus material leaves no stone unturned and no question unanswered. The truth vibrates from every page and once you have read it, your outlook on life will never be the same again. You will then realize that you are an eternal being living in a universe where the keynote is love. It is from this unrivalled material that we have the insight that we will share in the Nutshell series.

At this point in time there is a massive spiritual awakening taking place on this planet. This means that receptiveness for the Martinus material is growing every day. We can already see this in the shape of the many books that confirm aspects of what Martinus says, such as the near-death experience, children who spontaneously talk about past lives, people who are relieved from life-debilitating traumas via regression therapy, people who hear or are greeted by loved ones who have passed over, people who see visions of the afterlife on their deathbeds and many more. It is as if the spiritual world is knocking on the 'door' of the physical world saying: hey, I'm here! Look at me, heed me, study me, learn about me…. I am not going to go away.

In this book we will look at the question of whether reincarnation is more than just a belief. Our respective ´jobs´ are: Else will explain what Martinus says about the subject. She is Danish and has been studying the Martinus material for over 23 years. Maria will supplement what Martinus says with examples from life here on the physical plane. In this way we will have knowledge from above and from below. As the two fit like a hand in a glove, it is not easy to dismiss the truth of what you are about to read.

Enjoy!

But before we proceed, Maria explains how we met and how this project came about:

I have always loved reading books that stretch my knowledge beyond what I know, shed further light on what I think I already know, or make me question what I do know. Else's books, and the astonishing work of Martinus, have filled my desire for knowledge beyond my wildest imaginings. That's why, after reading 'Death Is an Illusion', I promptly downloaded all her books, reached out to her on Facebook, and realized that she lived just 30 minutes' drive from where I live in Spain. I simply had to meet her, and we became firm friends. It still amazes me that the Universe placed us both in such close proximity to each other. Serendipity? Absolutely!

During the years of our friendship, we've had many long and interesting talks about Martinus and the profound insights we've learned from his work, so it was with the greatest pleasure that I agreed to work with Else on the 'Nutshell Series'. Else liked the perspective I could bring, having read my own two books, and knowing that I am so passionate about personal development and spirituality. This is our first team effort and we are very excited to share it with you. At the end of each chapter that Else has written, I will add my own humble opinion of how I see the work impacting us and the profound effects it can have on how we live our lives today. These I'll call Points to Ponder, and I invite you, the reader, to reflect on your own points and ponder what impact Martinus' work could have in your life.

What struck me when I first learned of Martinus was this: How was it possible that this illegitimate, uneducated man who had no access to knowledge beyond a couple of books, could come up with insights and knowledge of cosmology that is astonishing even in 2018? He had no access to the internet, and no one, not even the greatest minds of the 20th century, have ever come close to formulating a whole world picture that is both deeply spiritual and entirely logical. This profound knowledge can only have come from a higher source... a different realm where all knowledge exists and which we humans on earth have barely even glimpsed. When you think of child prodigies... who are born with incredible musical and artistic talents... where did they get them? Where indeed! I believe Else's books and the work of Martinus can leave little doubt in our minds that the only logical explanation is that we reincarnate time and time again. I hope that by the end of this book, you'll embrace the logic of it yourself.

Table of Contents

1. Introduction

Is Reincarnation more than Wishful Thinking?

Would it not be wonderful if we did not only live one life? Would it not be great to know that death was an illusion and that we lived on after our physical body had stopped functioning? If we could know that death was not the end of life, would that not make us much less worried or afraid, make us much more confident and happier? If we could simply with one stroke eliminate all fear of death, would that not give our lives a whole new meaning and perspective?

The point in time where we can say that reincarnation is much more than wishful thinking is now. Now we have the evidence, the underlying theory and the logical basis for saying that we do not only live one life. To us, the authors of this book, reincarnation is not a belief and it is not wishful thinking. It is a fact. We have studied this theme for more than 20 years and there is not a shadow of a doubt to us that we live on after the death of the physical body. We are also completely convinced that we come back to the physical plane again and again. We have lived many lives before this one and we are going to live many lives after this. Our present life is just one in a series of lives that we live here on Earth. And in this book, we are going to present the arguments, the logic and the evidence for these claims.

This small book is your exit key from the one-life theory. This book will make you see the sublime logic in reincarnation, it will show you how reincarnation takes place and it will present the evidence. It will reveal the reasons why it simply makes no sense to live only once. We are also going to reveal where we go when we pass over, what happens there, and how we choose our new parents. At the end of the book you are going to be convinced that you are an eternal being on an everlasting journey through physical and spiritual realms in a universe where the basic tone is love.

There is one important point that we have to make here: When we reincarnate, we move forward in evolution. This means that for each life we live, we become a better, wiser, more moral and intelligent version of ourselves. We get a finer, more advanced and beautiful human body. It is impossible to reincarnate into subhuman species such as rats, snakes or the like. This misconception seems to flourish among eastern religions, but it is neither logical nor indeed possible to reincarnate into species that are completely foreign to our own genetic basis. Even in the west, most people who have not studied reincarnation, will associate it with 'coming back to Earth as a cat, dog or whatever'. When you have read this book, you will know that this is not possible, and you will come to understand that in your next life you will be a more evolved human being than you are in this life.

Death is nothing more than a break from our physical experience of life and it is valid to compare it with sleep. When we sleep, we also leave our physical body in order for basic repairs to take place, and when we wake up, we are still the same person and we continue our life from the point where we went to sleep last night. In principle death is the same. We leave the old or injured physical body behind and when we reincarnate and get a new body, we continue our development from where it stopped when we passed over. Death is like a long sleep and when we reincarnate and 'wake up' we simply continue our journey from exactly the same place where it ended when we 'fell asleep'. We are on a continuous journey towards perfection, and each life is one step on that journey. We are eternal beings, so there is no hurry and we cannot get the journey wrong. The journey is about our creation of experience.

Fifty years ago, it was mostly Buddhists and Hinduists who believed in reincarnation, but this is changing rapidly. Today the idea that we live more than once is spreading beyond the boundaries of the traditional religions; indeed, you do not have to belong to any religion to be convinced that reincarnation is more than just a belief.

In traditional Christian countries such as Sweden, Norway and Denmark, one third of the population believes in reincarnation, and they do so without being bothered by the fact that Christianity does not support the idea. Many people are leaving the traditional religions because they feel that the old evangelical way of looking at life does not cater for modern people living in a society with a scientific outlook. They feel that there is more to life than what is written in the scriptures, and that traditional religion may not have all the answers to life's big questions.

However, you cannot delve into the question of reincarnation if you base your knowledge solely on what the materialistic sciences have to offer. They really have little or nothing to offer in this respect, and it is clear that when you move away from what can be seen, measured and weighed, you approach a level about which the materialistic sciences know nothing. The materialistic sciences are not concerned with the spiritual level of existence.

2

But in order to have a basis from which you can explore reincarnation, you need a spiritual approach. As already mentioned in the foreword our main source of spiritual insight is the work of Martinus (1890 - 1981), the 20th century Danish intuitive and mystic. Through two profound spiritual experiences at the age of 30, Martinus experienced an expansion of his consciousness and it soon became clear that he had achieved cosmic consciousness. He was able to see beyond the physical level and into the spiritual level, where everything has its origin. And the thing is, we cannot answer the big questions about life after death and reincarnation based only on our materialistic sciences.

Our materialistic sciences can only answer questions of a physical nature, and that is what they are meant to do. They were never meant to deal with spiritual aspects of life. The spiritual aspects cannot be weighed and measured as physical matter can, and as the spiritual level is not accessible to our physical senses, our materialistic sciences will never be able to shed light on spiritual aspects. In order to do that, we need people who have spiritual insight. And that is exactly what Martinus had. He had the energy of intuition under the control of his will and this means that whenever he focused his thoughts on a question, the answer came to him immediately. Based on his intuitive ability he became the author of more than 10.000 pages of spiritual wisdom. It is the most complete spiritual guidance ever revealed to humankind and it is still not very well known. Actually, we can say that it is the world's best kept secret. The reason may well be that Martinus was Danish and all his work was written in Danish. His work is in the process of being translated into a large number of languages, but in its entirety, it can, at the present time, only be read in Danish. Else is Danish and she has studied Martinus´ work since 1995, when she, much to her surprise, encountered the material. It is an understatement to say that she was enthusiastic. She was red-hot with excitement and this is her 7th book about aspects of Martinus´ work.

The work of Martinus is also called "The Third Testament" and it constitutes new directions from the divine plane of existence to humankind. It is the long-awaited sequel to "The New Testament". The new directions to humankind are logical, and they are completely fitted to our present level of evolution. They appeal to our intellects and not so much to our feelings. They answer all the big questions about life, death and the mystery of both. They explain where we are coming from and where we are going, why there is no death, why reincarnation is much more than a religious belief, how we can shape our fate when we become knowledgeable about the law of karma, what the structure of life is, how evolution and creation walk hand in hand, and what the master plan of life is. The work of Martinus is an inexhaustible source of spiritual wisdom and it surpasses everything that has been revealed about spirituality until now.

Despite being called "The Third Testament", the work of Martinus is not an object of faith and it is not a basis for a new religion. It is not something we should believe in. It is something that we should study and then see if it fits with what we can observe in the world. It is a supplement to life's own speech. When we have a certain amount of experience in our mental 'rucksack', we have become quite good at understanding life's own speech, and at that point we will succumb to the penetrating logic of Martinus' work. We will then see that what Martinus reveals is a complete world picture based on logic and intelligence. A world picture can only be complete when it explains both the physical and the spiritual levels of existence. If we only look at the physical level, as we mostly do today, we only have half a world picture. We shall reveal the complete world picture at the end of this book. The work of Martinus is a basis for a merger of science and spirituality. Science and spirituality have to come together to make our world picture complete.

In this book we shall concentrate on the concept of reincarnation because it is of paramount importance to our understanding of life on this planet. Martinus clearly says that reincarnation is the basis for life on Earth. All life forms reincarnate, from atoms, molecules and cells, via organs, plants, animals, human beings to planets and galaxies. The world is a much more magical place than most people think, and, in this book, we are going to lift a small corner of the veil that covers this big magic.

Points to Ponder from Maria:

I do believe that this small book *is* your 'exit key from the one-life theory', as Else suggests in the introduction. Whilst I believe that everyone has the right to choose what they believe, and they believe such for their own unique set of reasons and life path during this particular lifetime, when I am challenged by people who are total non-believers of anything beyond this life, who tell me such thoughts are the product of a fanciful and wild imagination, I often ask 'But is it not better to believe that this could be true, than to believe there is nothing at all? What do you have to lose by believing that there could be a world of magic beyond what you can see, feel, hear, touch and taste in this life?' What do you, the reader, think?

As children, we were told fairy tales, and believed in Santa. As we grew up, we immersed ourselves in fantasy and science-fiction movies and films. Why? Could it be because a part of us knows that there is more to the world than meets our limited senses? I believe we're all born with the knowledge that there is more but that knowledge is systematically bred out of most of us as we grow up. We become shaped by what society tells us is true, and too many people never stop to question it. But more and more people *are* starting to question it and the spiritual shift that Martinus talks about is already taking place. If you are reading this book, then you, dear reader, are part of that shift. You are asking questions. You believe, or want to believe, that there is more to life than just *this* life.

Else also mentions in the introduction that we evolve with each lifetime, and that in our next life, we will be more evolved than we are in this one. I became a vegetarian when I was 32. Nobody in my world at that time was a 'veggie' and I was considered pretty freaky. Everyone wanted to argue with me about why it was normal, natural and necessary to eat meat. But I had made up my mind and absolutely nothing anyone could have said could have changed it. But why? Why did I feel so utterly compelled to become a vegetarian? Why was I so moved by the plight of animals being slaughtered in their 1000s (now multi-millions), that I simply refused to be part of this mass slaughter any longer? Within my passion about this there had to be an explanation, a reason. I was at a loss to understand it, beyond just knowing at a deep soul level, that it was wrong for me to ever eat animals again.

But the explanation I had long sought became clear to me from reading Else's work. I had somehow learned in a previous life that all animals are sacred in the eyes of the creator, and I carried that knowledge into this life with me. It didn't surface until I was in my early 30s (an age which Martinus also explains is the age where we pick up the threads where we left off in our previous life). Nothing else had ever made more sense to me.

But we can of course learn more compassion in this life and we should always strive to, by looking for the truth, examining our values, our conscience, researching the realities of what goes on in our world, and making new decisions and choices from there. This is one way of evolving in this lifetime. What area of your life could benefit from closer examination of your own feelings and morals? Give it some thought and you might be surprised at what comes up for you. You may not decide to become a vegetarian of course, but you may decide to have a meat-free day once a week, or to shop for meat that comes from more humane sources. Even the smallest step you take counts towards your evolution. Every loving thought you have, every small act of kindness, all get added to your spiritual 'bank' account. So ponder how you might add more credit to your bank account every day for the rest of your life, and your higher self will thank you when your spirit leaves your body and goes back to the other side for a rest, before bringing you back into a new body and a new lifetime of evolution.

2. The Spirit

Today the one-life theory has a firm hold on the majority of people living in the western world, but the idea that we only live one life has never been proved. The idea that our consciousness is extinguished when the body dies is impossible to prove. Indeed, this idea is closely linked to the idea that we *are* our body. Many people think that we arose out of the egg and sperm cells at conception and that our existence will be annulled when we die. They think we come from just those two cells and will return to nothing. But that is an explanation that is way too simple. The two sex cells cannot create a new body without the presence of a spirit. We have to understand that we are not just our physical body, but spiritual beings having an experience of the Earth plane in a perishable physical body. The physical body is not who we are, it is merely our 'space suit' or vehicle for our temporary visit here.

The physical body is 'just' an instrument for our spirit, and in order to understand what the spirit is, we shall have a look at the 'ingredients' of the spirit: our I, our consciousness and our life force.

But before we do that, we must realize that there is more to the world than what we can see and touch. We must realize that there is such a 'thing' as invisible, spiritual matter. Martinus calls this type of matter ray-formed matter but it really is the same as energy.

Ray-formed matter

Martinus calls energy ray-formed matter. It is an invisible, but measurable type of matter whose existence is in no way questioned by the science of physics. The science of physics calls this type of matter electromagnetic radiation and it is well described and understood. However, many people still cringe when they hear that invisible matter exists and they refuse to believe it. But that is only until their smart phone rings. Or until they start roaming to get information from the Internet.

All our cordless devices work because there is such a 'thing' as ray-formed matter or electromagnetic radiation. When our smart phone rings, it is because it has a specific wavelength that it operates on and the device then pulls in the information held in the shape of the call we receive. If there were no such thing as ray-formed matter, we could never have cordless devices such as mobile phones, tablets, radios, televisions,

GPS etc. Nothing cordless would work if there were no electromagnetic radiation or ray-formed matter.

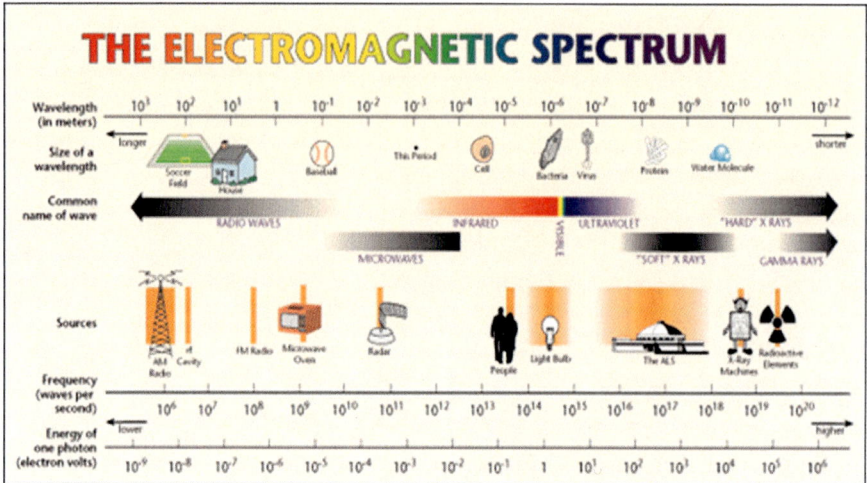

The electromagnetic spectrum is well defined by the science of physics and it operates on a huge range of wavelengths and frequencies.

Our devices work because ray-formed matter holds information. Energy or electromagnetic radiation is packed with information. We know that because it is no secret to modern humans that we get information out of the air when we roam on our iPad or speak on our smartphone.

The electromagnetic spectrum has a huge range of wavelengths and frequencies, so we are talking about a type of matter that has many ways of manifesting itself, ways that we have not yet fully understood. Ray-formed matter exists on many wavelengths. Some are well known and well defined, as illustrated in the drawing above, but this type of matter also exists on wavelengths that are so fine, that they have not been discovered yet.

Ray-formed matter is energy and energy is everywhere. It has now become clear that what we once thought of as empty space, is not empty at all. It is stuffed with energy. We shall see what the characteristics of energy are shortly.

Because of the constant use we make of this invisible type of matter, no modern, informed human being would claim that invisible matter does not exists. We all know that it does, because we make use of it every day.

In order to understand what our spirit / I / consciousness consist of, it is important to establish that invisible, ray-formed matter has a factual existence.

Our I

We all have an I. Nobody would deny that. There is an I inside all living beings. There is something inside us that experiences, that thinks and has a will. We experience this as the core of who we are, as the unit that gives us a sense of self. This unit is what decides what we do, it has the final say in our body.

We use the word I a lot. *"I just went on a holiday to Greece, I just had a shower, I just bought a new dress, I am crazy about pizza, I love you etc."* We all agree that we have something in us that we call I. We can also agree that what we call I is what we consider to be the core or essence of who we are.

But the materialistic science does not support the idea that we have an I. It claims that our sense of self or I is in the brain. It believes that we ARE our brain. Still it does not go around saying *"The brain just went on a holiday to Greece, the brain just had a shower, the brain just bought a new dress, the brain is crazy about pizza, the brain loves you etc."* That would be pure nonsense. And it is clear that even though the materialistic science says we have no I, we all use the term every day, so there is something amiss here, because obviously we have an I and nobody in their right mind would deny that. This I is the core of who we are, our sense of self, our sense of individuality. It is the I that decides what we do, because the I has a will.

But even if we dug forever in the physical body, we would be unable to find a physical thing that could be identified as our I. Our I does not consist of physical matter – it is a spiritual entity. We can also say that our I is the center of our spirit and around this center we have our consciousness. Our I and consciousness make up our spirit and this spirit consists of energy.

Energy is defined as a type of force, as something that can set things in motion. And energy cannot be dissolved or stop existing. Energy can change form, but according to the first law of thermodynamics, energy cannot cease to exist. For that reason, it must be considered as an eternally existing reality. Our spirit consists of energy and based on the just cited law it is not difficult to understand that we have an eternal entity in our spirit.

The spirit is a bubble of energy and it is identical to our consciousness. Our spirit and consciousness operate on a specific wavelength. Let us now look at what consciousness is.

Consciousness

Our consciousness is an electrical field holding our I and all the aspects that are typical of that I. Among these aspects we have a sense of having a self, the sense of being me, of having a core which we call I. Our consciousness also holds the totality of our thoughts, our memories, our intelligence, our character traits, our personality traits, our talents, our likes and dislikes, our emotions, our patterns of reaction, our habits and what we can find it in our heart to do to others, our level of compassion and universal love, our morals and the basis for our behavior. It also holds all the knowledge, conscious or unconscious, that we have accumulated. The knowledge we have accumulated forms the basis for all our decisions, so this knowledge is very important to our survival. The ingredients of our consciousness define who we are, indeed, they constitute the most important part. We *are* our consciousness, because it holds all the aspects that make us into the specific person we are.

The aspects that define our consciousness are real and factual, and nobody in his right mind would deny that. And yet *none* of these aspects are physical. We can dig forever in the physical body without finding a physical item in there that would be identical to our consciousness. Our sciences say that consciousness is in the brain and that it has arisen from processes in the brain. But that theory has never been proved. Nobody has been able to prove that consciousness arises in the brain. This theory has probably arisen because of a lack of a better explanation and a lack of knowledge about spiritual matter. Consciousness has so many aspects and is so unique to every human being that it cannot simply arise out of the 'rubbing together' of neurons inside the brain. No, in order to understand what consciousness really is, we have to include the idea of an invisible and electrical, but measurable type of matter. None of the 'ingredients', that define who we are, are physical. Yet it is obvious that we have them. Without them we wouldn't be who we are. They hold our I or self. The ingredients of our consciousness define our whole identity. Our consciousness and I are who we really are. We can also say that our consciousness and I are the main 'ingredients' of our spirit. The physical body is merely an instrument for the consciousness and I – an instrument that the consciousness or I uses as long as it functions.

Through the above it becomes clear that we cannot define who we are only on the basis of the physical ingredients. If we do not add the spiritual aspects to who we are, we are left with only inert physical material. We cannot define who we are without taking the consciousness or spirit into account. Yet, the materialistic viewpoint states that consciousness is derived entirely from physical matter, indeed that it is a by-product of the functioning of the brain. It's unclear, though, exactly how this could work as it is very hard to get consciousness out of non-consciousness.

Our consciousness does not sit in the brain, but it sits as a bubble that surrounds and permeates the whole body, i.e. in the aura. We shall have a look at how this can be substantiated, but first we should analyze the main ingredient in our consciousness: thoughts.

What are thoughts?

We all know that we have a lot of thoughts milling around in our head. We cannot see our thoughts and we cannot grab them and hold them in our hand, but we know that they are there. They are an invisible part of us, but a very important one, as our thoughts are behind everything we do, say and are.

It is important to understand that our thoughts, in spite of being invisible, have a tangible, physical aspect. They are measurable. When electrodes are placed on the head of a person, thought activity can be measured. Thoughts are measurable, because they are small electrical currents.

And now we come to an aspect that is not well understood but which is nonetheless irrefutable: <u>Our thoughts are small bundles of energy as well as carriers of information.</u> Our thoughts do both: they hold information and they hold energy. The information-carrying aspect of a thought is only one side of it. The other side is that a thought also holds energy. This means that a thought has a double identity: it holds information and it holds energy. A thought is like a coin with two sides. One side holds energy and the other side holds information. The two cannot be separated.

There is energy in our thoughts. With energy we can move things, we can make things work and function. This means that a thought is a small bundle of energy. Our thoughts are much more important than has hitherto been supposed. The totality of our thoughts holds a lot of energy and this energy is our life force.

The Life Force

It is the energy of our life force that makes us alive. It is the presence of our life force that constitutes the difference between a dead body and one that is alive. Our life force is of an electrical nature. We can also think of it as a magnetic field. We are electrical beings, and it is this electricity that makes it possible for us to lift our limbs, to blink an eyelid and to breathe. It is the electricity in our life force that makes our hearts beat and our bowels move etc. As soon as the life force leaves the body, the body can no longer move because there is no more electricity.

The physical body is a mere instrument for the life force. At this point it should be pointed out that the life force is constituted by thoughts and thoughts constitute our consciousness and our consciousness holds our I. So, we have a pretty package holding thoughts, consciousness, life force and our I. We can call this package our spirit. Our spirit is an electrical entity that holds all the information about who we are. It *IS* who we are.

As we just pointed out, our physical body is an instrument. The reason why it is easy to see that the body is just an instrument lies in the fact that there is no physical difference between a dead body and a body that is alive. Both have exactly the same physical ingredients: skin, muscles, hair, skeleton, heart, liver, lungs, kidneys, eyes, ears, mouth etc. If the physical ingredients of the two are identical, then how can it be that one is dead and the other is alive? It is obviously not the physical ingredients that make the body come alive. It is the spirit.

When the field of electricity or spirit has been pulled out of the body, the body has been deprived of its source of energy, and as any other electrical instrument it does not work without electricity. It is dead without its energy source. This can be seen when the flat line appears on the screen of the monitoring devices that are used in hospitals. When the flat line appears, the body has been deprived of its source of energy and we say that it is dead.

The body dies when it is no longer a useful instrument for the spirit. As the body is a physical thing, it is subject to wear and tear. As we live our lives on the physical plane, our body gets worn and we age. At a certain point the body is no longer a suitable instrument for the experience of the physical plane on behalf of the I / spirit, so it pulls out and we say that the body is dead. But it is only dead inasmuch as its source of energy has been pulled out. Because it was the spirit that held the physical ingredients of the body together, the body will start to dissolve and rot as soon as the spirit leaves. But for the spirit it is a great thing to release itself from the body when it is no longer in working condition.

For that reason, it is great to die and something that we can all look forward to. Death simply means that we have been released from the physical body that can no longer serve us. Death is a principle of instrument replacement. After a rest we will start the process of replacing the old body with a new one. Until we have created a new physical body, we shall live for a while in our spiritual body. But as the spiritual body holds all the ingredients that define who we are, as we ARE indeed our spirit body, we will feel exactly the same as we did before. Only now, we are lighter and freer, as we no longer have the physical body to drag around.

Who we are is our spirit, we are NOT our physical body. This point is hugely important.

Is it possible to substantiate that we have a spirit and that this spirit / consciousness / life force / I actually sits around the body? Indeed, it is. The energy field of the spirit can be visualized in our aura.

The Aura

All living beings have an aura. Some people can see auras, but even though it may be invisible to most people, the aura can be photographed and measured using modern equipment. The energy field of our spirit is an electrical entity, and because it consists of energy, its existence can be substantiated by science.

Our aura is identical to our consciousness. We can say that the existence of our consciousness gets an almost-physical expression in our aura. When we look at an aura, we see a visible reflection of our consciousness. As we can see, our consciousness is not limited to the brain, as is the main-stream idea today. Our consciousness sits as a bubble around and inside the physical body. This bubble is who we really are: a field of energy holding all the information about who we are.

In 1939 the Russian inventor Semyon Davidovitch Kirlian found out that the energies of the aura could be photographed using a specific technique. This means that we can now actually have our auras photographed. There is no doubt that the energy field of our consciousness / I / life force exists, because now it can be photographed, and we can see that we have an energy field or aura around our body.

When to this we add the fact that a dead body has no aura, it becomes clear that the difference between a dead body and one that is alive is the existence of the aura or consciousness around the body that is alive. The presence of the electrical field is what determines the difference between alive and dead. When we die, the flat line appears on the screen of the monitoring devices at hospitals and this also means that the energy field has left the physical body.

Human aura photographed using the Kirlian technology

The ´Package´

So, let us sum up what the ´pretty package´ of the spirit consists of. The I / consciousness / life force constitute our spirit. The spirit can be visualized in the aura. The spirit is who we really are. This means that we are primarily spiritual beings – beings whose whole identity consists of spiritual, electrical forces. We always have our spiritual body. From time to time we also have a physical body in addition to our spiritual body. This happens when we incarnate our spirit or I into a physical body. A body that is alive is a body that has a spirit inside. When there is no spirit, the body is dead. Without the spirit the body would become a corpse, and it would start to dissolve almost immediately after the spirit had left.

All living beings have a spirit and this spirit is of a non-physical nature. It cannot be seen with the naked eye and it cannot be weighed. But its existence can be substantiated when we use modern apparatus, because we can measure and photograph that there is an electrical field around a body that is alive and none around a dead body. In the spirit lies all the information about who we are. We ARE our spirit; we are NOT our physical body. Our spirit is an independent entity that exists whether it is connected to a physical body or not.

The Magnet

Our spirit is also a magnet. A magnet attracts things. This means that we attract people, circumstances, events, occurrences with our spirit. It is the law of attraction that is at work here. Let us look at how this works.

Because our spirit is of an electrical nature, it has a specific vibration. Everything has a specific vibration. All spirits are different because the spiritual matter contained in the spirit is different. The spiritual matter of the consciousness mainly consists of thoughts. A happy thought is different from a sad thought. Because thoughts are different, they also have different vibrations. In the same way as it is differences in vibration that determine whether a color is red or blue, it is also the content of the thought that will determine the vibration of any specific thought. A happy thought has a different vibration to a sad thought. Because our thoughts are small bundles of energy, the contents of the thoughts will determine their vibration. This vibration operates on a specific wavelength. The specific wavelength of our spirit is defined by the type of thoughts we think or allow to predominate in our mentality or consciousness.

This is an extremely important point, because when we know that, we can actively influence the wavelength of our consciousness. With positive thoughts our consciousness will operate on a wavelength that is different from the one it would have if we mainly thought negative thoughts. Positive thoughts will result in one wavelength and negative thoughts will result in a different wavelength. But these wavelengths are also small magnets. This is an even more important point. It means that we can decide what we attract with the type of thoughts we think. With positive thoughts we attract positive aspects of life and with negative thoughts we attract negative aspects of life. When we think positive thoughts, we will attract positive people into our life and with negative thoughts we will attract negative people. In this way we have a huge say in what we attract into our life. Martinus says that: *"Every human being is like a magnet that attracts exactly the events and people that can bring him / her the experiences most needed at the moment"* (Martinus: Two life elements (article)). When we actively work on improving our mix of thoughts, we will attract more positive aspects than if we did nothing.

But not only that: with positive thoughts we magnetize our blood positively and create a healthy body and with negative thoughts we magnetize our blood negatively and create illnesses. This is worth remembering, because this is something that we can to some extent decide ourselves. We can choose which thoughts we think. Our I has the final say about which thoughts are thought in our consciousness, so making a conscious decision about nurturing positive thoughts is of paramount importance to our overall wellbeing. The vibration and wavelength of our consciousness is determined by the type of thoughts we think. A consciousness filled with negative thoughts will operate on a wavelength that is different to the consciousness that is filled with positive thoughts.

It also means that the wavelengths of a terrorist will be very different to that of a very loving person. The consciousnesses of all living beings operate on a huge range of wavelengths. We are all very different, not only in looks, age and sex, but more importantly in our wavelengths. This means that the wavelength of our consciousness is a very important factor in what happens to us. We attract people, circumstances and occurrences with our wavelength. Our wavelength is decided by our I. Our I is the most important ingredient in us. Our I is the supreme ruler of our body. Our I determines our wavelength and our point of attraction.

This also means that it is a very good idea to be conscious about what type of thoughts we think. This aspect is not a minor one. It determines our life.

How Do we Know that Thoughts Are Important?

Some people may say that thoughts are not important, and it does not matter what we think. But that is certainly not true. This can be substantiated by the following observation:

When we look at all the man-made things that are around us, we know that they all, every one of them, no exception, started as a thought. The thought always precedes the physical manifestation. A chair, a house, a table, a car, a computer…you name it… started as a thought. The thought may have arisen from a physical need, like a desire for something to sit on when you were tired, or an idea for improvements to human life, such as houses, cars, computers and aeroplanes. They all started as a thought. Then the thought was probably transferred to paper in the shape of a drawing and only then was it created in physical matter. All man-made physical objects started as a thought. They were then manifested in physical matter. We can also say that all man-made things on the planet are manifested or materialised thoughts. There is no exception to this. We live in a world of materialized thoughts.

This process of creation is also valid on a higher level. Indeed, the whole physical world is materialized thoughts just as all manmade things are. The physical universe is the materialized thoughts of a higher being, God. This will be substantiated in the last chapter about the master plan of life.

Now we shall see what goes on with the spirit once it has pulled out of the physical body.

When the Life Force Leaves the Body

So, what happens to the spirit package when it leaves the body? Is it simply dissolved? No, the electricity or energy does not cease to exist just because it is no longer attached to the physical body. This is no different than with any other electrical device. When we unplug our lamp, we know that the electricity does not cease to exist either.

The field of energy of our life force is not dissolved just because it is no longer attached to a physical body. According to the first law of thermodynamics, also called the law of conservation of energy, the total energy of an isolated system remains constant. This law means that energy can neither be created nor destroyed. As the science of physics clearly states that energy cannot be destroyed, this means that we are standing on firm and solid scientific ground when we say that the energy field of our spirit is not dissolved or destroyed at death. It is no longer at work in the physical body it inhabited before, but it is still there. In a later chapter we shall explore what happens to the spirit once it has released itself from the physical body.

Now we shall explore a very important aspect of who we are: our talents.

Talents

A very important aspect of our consciousness are our talents. We are all born with a lot of talents. Some people are good at singing, some are good at painting, some at playing a musical instrument, at dancing, cooking, baking, writing, speaking foreign languages, making woodwork, felling trees, speaking in public, teaching, learning, understanding mathematics, skating, running, hiking, climbing, fighting, caring for the sick, communicating, designing, programming, being innovative, making money etc. etc. There is no end to the various talents people have.

But where do the talents come from? Do we just inherit them from our parents, as is the general understanding? No, we do not. It simply cannot be like that, because a lot of us have talents that none of our parents have. If a talent is not shared by the parents or the grandparents, then where does it come from? Science has no answer to where our talents come from, if they are not shared with the parents or ancestors.

But Martinus is very clear about this: we have worked hard to get the talents we have. There is only one way to become good at something and that is to practice. We know that when we practice something, no matter how hard we found it to begin with, we will eventually become better at it. The more we practice, the better we get. At the end, we find the thing we have practiced so easy, that we cannot understand how we once found it difficult.

Martinus explains it like this: When we start taking an interest in something and start practicing it, a small spiritual 'kernel' is created in our consciousness. This is a talent kernel. The more we practice, the stronger and larger does the talent kernel get. The skills we have performed a number of times are saved in the talent kernel, so that we do not have to start the learning process all over again each time we practice. The talent kernel is like a small memory chip that can hold the information about how a certain thing is performed. The more we practice, the more information is stored in the memory chip. When the memory chip is full, we have become virtuosos at performing the specific task. We then have a huge talent for this specific activity.

A talent is something that we have created ourselves through practice. It is not something that we have inherited from our parents. We take our talents with us from life to life, because they are stored in our fate element.

The Fate Element

The information in the talent kernel is stored in our fate element, which forms part of our supra-consciousness. The fate element holds all the information we have acquired through practice all through our former lives, so the fate element holds a lot of talent kernels. It can be likened to a 'container' for a lot of memory chips. When we pass over, we take our fate element with us. The fate element is like a storage 'device' where everything we have learned is saved. This storage device is full of talent kernels from all the skills we have practiced through our many lives. Some talent kernels are so fat that the skill they hold has reached the level of perfection, some are less fat and the skill they hold may only have reached the medium level, but still it is there, and we can continue working on the skill in our next incarnation.

This means that we do not lose the abilities we have worked hard to become good at when we die. We take all our talents with us. The fate element is where we keep them, and it accompanies us from life to life. It is a storeroom for all our talents and abilities. But not only for our talents and abilities but for everything we are: our personality, our level of intelligence, our level of development, our likes and dislikes, our habits, our humanity, our character traits etc. Also, our scars, physical as well as mental, are stored in the fate element. A very dramatic experience in a past life can throw its shadows into the next life and can cause traumas and mental disorders. If we are born with severe traumas that have no apparent cause in the present life, they are certainly 'scars' inflicted to the psyche in a past incarnation. These can be a very heavy burden for the person, but the good news is that they can be greatly alleviated during past life regression therapy.[1]

Also, physical scars can be stored in the fate element and transferred to the next physical body. Examples of this are birthmarks and discolorations to the skin like 'café au lait' spots, 'salmon patches' or port-wine stains. When these scars are transferred to the next body it is because they were caused by a major trauma that did not have time to heal properly before the person passed over.

Under the Evidence chapter we shall look at some examples of mental as well as physical traumas.

Phobias and Fears

Many phobias and fears also have their origin in a past life. We can have lived through situations that led to an early death, so such an event may have imprinted itself so vehemently on our psyche that it may take several incarnations to get completely over it. If, for example, we were drowned in a past life, then this may well result in a fear of being on lakes or the sea; if we fell off a cliff in a past life, this can give rise to a fear

---

[1] *Regression Therapy: Through trance or hypnosis the patient is taken to a time when the cause of the present trauma originated. This will in most cases be a former life. Regression therapy has a huge healing potential and thousands of people have been relieved from life-debilitating traumas via this method. Hundreds of books have been published about this highly interesting healing method.*

of heights and if we starved in a previous life, this can give rise to an extreme focus on food which may well lead to obesity, or simply strange patterns of eating or anorexia / bulimia. So many phobias and fears, indeed most of them, have their roots in previous lives. The good news is that they can be healed via regression therapy.

Traditional science, particularly in the mental health and psychology fields, has done much to understand how phobias are formed and how they can be healed in your current lifetime. However, it does not and cannot provide all the answers. Phobias and irrational fears that show up in this life can have their roots in past lives, and many past life therapists, such as Dr Brian Weiss, have provided compelling evidence attesting to this. When absolutely no reason for such fears can be found in one's existing life, journeying back into a past life can often provide the answers.

Everything we have become at the time we pass over is stored in the fate element and we take everything that life has taught us to become with us into our next life. It is this sum of who we have become that marks our progress in evolution and it is not so, that we have to start from scratch each time we enter into a new physical body. We take the totality of who we are with us each time we pass over, and after a rest on the spiritual plane, we take the accumulated contents of our fate element with us into our next life. Nothing of what we have become at our time of death is lost.

We build on the accumulated talents and wisdom in our next life and in that way, we evolve in wisdom, intelligence and know-how for each life we live. Our many lives on earth can be likened to climbing a huge staircase. Each life is a step up that staircase. For each step up, we have become a better, wiser, more tolerant and all-loving being. Some have come higher on the staircase than others, but we are all relentlessly climbing that staircase. At the end of the staircase we find perfection, so in that sense we can say that we are all subject to being perfected. Later in this book we shall see what else is at the end of that staircase.

Our fate element, the 'container' of our accumulated wisdom and talents 'sits' in the energy field of our consciousness or spirit.

What survives death and what reincarnates is the package of the spirit. We shall soon have a closer look at how the actual process of reincarnation takes place, but before we do that we shall look at another interesting aspect of the role our spirit plays within the same lifetime.

The greatest factor in who we are today is who we were before, what we have been through, what we have suffered and learned, what we have practiced and experienced.

Points to Ponder from Maria:

Re. Ray-formed matter

After reading this chapter, can we really still believe that we live only one life? I don't see how anyone rationally can believe it, as Else so clearly shows us the difference between a dead body and a live one. This might seem obvious until you really stop and think about it. The body, logically, has to be the house for the spirit, and the spirit must have come from another realm to inhabit the body at the moment of conception.

Thoughts cannot be seen or proven to exist, yet every human being on the planet knows that his or her life is governed by every thought that s/he has, so we don't need to 'prove' their existence to know that they are not only real, they are the custodians of every single thing we do. The thought connects in the brain and the brain instructs the body to act. Action follows thought; stand up, sit down, speak, laugh, go get food… all of it is governed by thought. Else mentions that activity can be measured by means of electrodes placed on the head, and that with energy we can move things, make things work and function.

An interesting and fun experiment you can try at home to prove to yourself that your thoughts have power and can influence objects, is to get a pendulum and tie it to the end of a string. You can do this with a washer or any piece of metal that has a hole in the middle. I've even done it recently with a locket and chain. I undid the chain and let the locket dangle at the end with the large claw clasp. It worked a treat.

Here's what you do

1. Rest your arm on your thigh or an armchair (arm), and hold the end of the string or chain between your thumb and forefinger.
2. Steady the object. I do this by saying 'Be still' a few times over until it becomes completely still. I am saying everything in my mind, concentrating on what the object needs to do.
3. Now ask it to swing clockwise for yes. It will swing within a few seconds.
4. Ask it to be still again.
5. Now ask it to swing counterclockwise for no.

Almost without fail, the object will respond to these commands. You can then take it to the next level by asking it questions that matter to you and for which you are seeking a clear answer. For example, you have two job offers and don't know which one to take. I believe that your subconscious always knows more than you do, so using this method you can tap into the wisdom of your subconscious by asking it which job you should take.

To do this you always need to give it clear instructions on the question and answer. So for example, you'd have job 1 and job 2. You would ask 'Should I take job 1?' and think about that job. You are waiting for a yes or no from the object. After a short while, it will be clearly swinging clockwise, or counterclockwise. You can double check your answer then by asking 'Should I take job 2?' and almost certainly, the answer will correspond correctly to whatever the first answer was; ie, if job 1 was yes, job 2 will be no.

You can have a lot of fun with this, asking it all kinds of questions!

The idea of ray-formed matter may sound a little far-fetched, but again, the way Else explains it leaves us in no doubt that it exists because we are using it every day now in our lives. At one time, not that long ago, the concept of being able to talk to someone over the phone (or a computer!) while being able to see them live on screen was a fantasy – a science fiction idea that was kind of fun to think about, but it was never going to be a reality. Just as the earth was believed to be flat. People really thought that if you sailed too far you would fall off the edge of the earth. That seems silly to us now, because we know so much more. The time will come, I believe, when Martinus' work will become common knowledge and truth that is accepted as fact… just like how we now accept that the world is round.

Re: Our I

Although I have believed in past lives for a long time, I nonetheless felt a disconnect between my 'now' self – my 'I', and my past-life selves. It is only recently that the reality sunk in, again after reading over much of Else's work in preparation for this book, that I am who I am and have always been… I don't remember who I was, but who I was and who I am now is the *same spirit*, evolved into who I am now. It is exactly the same for you, and every one of us on this planet today. I urge you to really think about this!

When you realize that the good and bad parts of who you are is the result of the many lives you've lived, this brings a feeling of unconditional love to your inner being – the being that is eternal, immortal, and who seeks only to evolve to joy, love and harmony in this life.

In the same vein, if you are suffering emotional or physical trauma in this life, this can be an indication that you need to learn new lessons in order to help yourself truly heal. I am absolutely convinced that emotional trauma we have suffered in past lives, if unresolved, will show up in our present life. Truly healing such pain generally means delving deep into your soul to find self-love, acceptance for all that you are, for all that you have suffered, and learning to love and forgive yourself to the point that you are ready to release your pain.

I think that Else's additional explanations about Consciousness, Thoughts, The Life Force, The Aura, and The 'Package', provide a solid spiritual rationale for how the threads of our very existence knit together. Can you find any loopholes? Anything that doesn't make sense, dear reader? I know that I can't.

Re: The Magnet

The Magnet explains what you may be familiar with as the Law of Attraction. If this is of interest and you'd like to read more, I recommend checking out Else and my book bundle on Amazon, both of which go into great detail about different aspects of the Law of Attraction.

Re: Talents

For me, one of the most convincing components of Else's work is that of talents: how and why we got ours? This is something that had long baffled me, especially when you see a child prodigy and wonder how they can play like maestros or sing like opera divas… but it makes perfect sense that in past lives, they had a passion for their craft, they studied, practiced and honed it and they bring that knowledge with them into their next life. They have done this to the point that we see them as gifted, and indeed they are, but those gifts have only been acquired by lifetimes of practicing that which they love.

And what of our own, more 'mediocre' talents? I used to think I wasn't good at much, but I realized that this was negative thinking, because when we look deeply enough, we realize that we all have talents and are all good at something. Those things we love and are good at are there and we need to acknowledge them and embrace them, and if we are really passionate about them, we can continue practicing and improving those skills this time round. I often say I'd love to be good at cooking, but the fact is I'm not, and I have no passion for cooking. So it's not going to happen for me in this lifetime, and that's fine, because it's not meant to. I'm ok with that. I focus on the things that I do love doing, and I get pleasure out of honing those skills. Reading, writing, helping people through my coaching… these are where my passions lie and I will spend the rest of this lifetime getting better at them all!

So, consider your own talents now, and think about how and why you love certain things. Does it not fascinate you that it is maybe because you learned similar skills in a previous lifetime? You may even have untapped talents waiting to be discovered so don't be afraid to try out new hobbies or games of skill or sports. There could be a genius hiding in you.

Re: The Fate Element / Phobias & Fears

Else discusses how scars, trauma and mental disorders can be caused by experiences we've had in past lives. As a Clinical Hypnotherapist I've had personal experience of this and seen people's lives changed when they were able to access past lives under hypnosis. One such incident I'd like to relay happened when I was attending a seminar to learn past life regression techniques, with world famous therapist Denise Lynn. She took the subject, a woman who was morbidly obese, into her past life and there it was discovered that in this particular life, fashion dictated that women had to wear very tight, boned corsets, bound up so tight at the back that it made breathing difficult. She practically starved herself so that she could fit into her dresses. Due to the pressure of the corset and lack of nutrition, she developed respiratory problems and died. At the end of her life, just before her death, Denise asked her what was the lesson she had learned in this lifetime that was affecting her current lifetime.

She said: "I swear I will never go hungry again!"

That vow had made such a powerful impact that it had surfaced in her in this lifetime, where she was terrified of dying from starvation. Consequently, she went the opposite way and ate much more than she needed. The woman was in tears when she came out of hypnosis and wanted to share something with the audience. She said *'I know that I lived that life. When I was asked to look down at my feet, I could see my feet! Due to my size these days, I have not seen my feet in so long, I don't know what they look like any more. But I know now what it is like to be slim, and to look down and see my feet. I understand now that I don't need that lesson anymore, that I won't starve, and that I can learn to eat normally.'*

Everyone in the room was moved and we all felt the profound emotional impact that the experience had on this woman, and I believe it changed her forever.

Phobias and fears are also very interesting to look at and whilst it's true that we can develop phobias in our current life at any time (usually as a result of a traumatic event or encounter with someone or something), again as a therapist I've experienced cases where we just couldn't find any cause in this life, which means that conventional therapeutic methods simply don't work. In such cases, past-life regression can uncover the truth about the phobia and then it can be released. The Fate Element as Else explains, makes it clear how and why this happens. Nothing we have learned or experienced is ever lost to us. It is with us for all time.

I normally do not suggest past-life regression to a client unless we have tried everything else and I'm sure there is no reason in this life. Then, it can be a very powerful therapeutic tool for healing. If this is an area of interest to you, then we definitely recommend you check out the work of Dr Brian Weiss, one of the world's leading authorities on the power of past life therapy to heal current life problems.

3. The Principle of Reincarnation

Cell Renewal

Our physical body consists of trillions of living cells. The number of cells alive in the body is difficult to define, because as we dig deeper and deeper into the ingredients of the body, we keep finding smaller and smaller units. Inside the cells there are molecules, and inside the molecules there are atoms and inside the atoms there are quarks and inside those there are hadrons and inside those there are protons and neutrons. There does not really seem to be a definite smallest unit because the deeper we dig, the more miniscule units we find. All the elements, of which our physical body has been built up, have a limited life span. The average life span of our cells is 3 months. Some live up to 6 months and some live only a few days. Then they die and are replaced by new cells. In that way our body is in a constant process of renewal. This process of renewal is valid for all the cells in our body: blood cells, muscle cells, lung cells, bone cells etc. Some cells renew themselves faster than others, but it is a scientific fact that after approximately a year all the cells of our body have been renewed.

This also goes for our brain cells. They also undergo a cycle of renewal. This point has been controversial because it has been believed that we had the same brain cells all through life. We somehow had to. Because if the brain cells were also renewed, then where was the constant element of our body? In the body there has to be a constant element, something that is always there despite the cell renewal. There has to be something that holds our identity, our memories and sense of self all though life. This constant element was believed to be the brain cells. Because if it was not the brain cells, and all other cells were replaced all the time, then where was the constant element in the body? This is quite impossible to explain if you believe that we ARE our physical bodies. As long as we think that we are identical to our physical body and consist only of physical matter, then we are at a loss to explain what constitutes the constant element of the body, if all our cells are renewed all the time.

But recent research states that also our brain cells are renewed. It is a group of scientists, headed by the neurologist Peter Eriksson, from Sahlgrenska Sjukhuset, Gothenburg, Sweden, who has shown that the creation of new nerve cells continues in certain parts of the human brain all through life.

So if we stick to the idea that we are identical to our physical body, we are now stuck with a body with no constant element. Such a body would be unable to remember anything beyond the life span of its brain cells. It would not only have no memories older than maybe 6 months, but it would also have no identity and sense of self. It would be an empty shell of physical material in a constant process of renewal.

The ongoing and constant renewal of our cells or physical matter means that after a year we have a completely new body. It may not look new and still it is undergoing a process of ageing, but the cells it consists of are new. All the cells that our body consisted of a year ago have been replaced by other cells. There is not a cell present in the body that was also there a year ago.

Let us look at 3 different photos of a person at different ages. We have chosen photos of Martinus, because he was photographed at different times in his life. On the first photo Martinus was 11 years old, on the second he was 30 years old and on the third he was 68 years old.

When you look at the 3 pictures, you see the same person at different ages. Yet, the 3 bodies do not have a single cell in common. Still we are looking at the same person, there is no doubt about that. The person is the same, but the bodies are different – they consist of physical matter that has been replaced by new in the space of time between when the pictures were taken. We are looking at 3 different bodies that do not have a single cell in common, not a tiny bit of physical matter in common. They are different bodies.

The Illusive Constant of the Physical Body

When it is at all possible to be the same person in 3 different bodies it is because who we are, the constant element of our body, is not of a physical nature. It is not physical. It is spiritual. The constant element of our body is the package of our spirit or consciousness, the field of energy that sits around the body as our aura, which we explained in the last chapter.

Once we take the spirit / consciousness / I into consideration, it is easy to explain how we can still be the same person even though we inhabit bodies that are under a constant process of renewal. The energy field of our consciousness holds all the information about who we are, and it is this field of information that constitutes the constant element of the body. The spirit cum consciousness holds all the characteristic of who we are. We ARE our spirit and not our body. We are first and foremost spiritual beings, not physical beings.

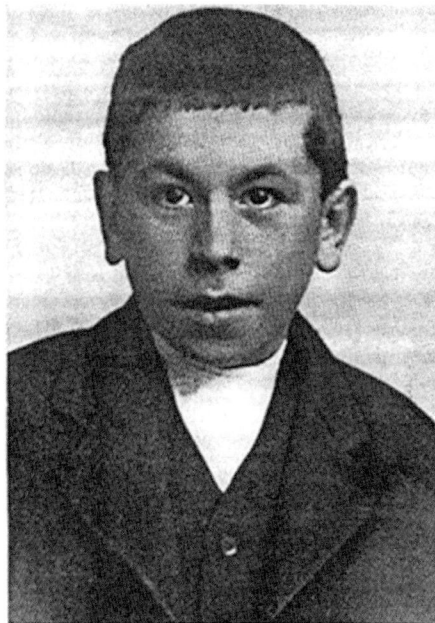

Martinus 11 years old

Martinus, 30 years old

MARTINUS 1958

Martinus, 68 years old

Our consciousness with our I and sense of self reincarnates on a constant basis into the ever-changing physical matter of the body. Reincarnation takes place many many times within the same lifetime. Reincarnation is nothing unusual. It is a prerequisite for life. Without reincarnation nothing would be alive.

The Butterfly

This can be substantiated even further if we look at the butterfly. This interesting insect makes use of 4 different bodies within one life time: first it dwells inside the egg, then it uses the body of a larva, then it inhabits the body of a chrysalis and finally it emerges in the body of a butterfly.

Butterfly eggs

Butterfly larva or caterpillar

Larva becoming a chrysalis

Butterfly emerging from the chrysalis

It is crystal clear that the butterfly uses 4 different bodies in one and the same lifetime. The bodies are different, but the butterfly is the same being. This is the principle of reincarnation made evident for all to see.

So, in nature we can see reincarnation illustrated in the magical transformation of the butterfly. The transformation of the butterfly can be said to be more dramatic than our own, because the butterfly changes most of its physical matter at one and the same time, whereas our reincarnation into the constantly renewed matter of the physical body is more gradual.

Our bodily renewal is still dramatic. In total, estimates of cell turnover in an adult human is about 50-70 billion per day. Most are the epithelial mucosal cells that line our digestive tract from mouth to anus. This means that more than 40 million cells are replaced per hour, 700.000 thousand per minute and more than 10 thousand per second. Quite a turnover!

The constant element of the physical body of any living being is its spirit or consciousness. The spirit delivers the energy necessary to sustain life. The energy of the spirit / consciousness / I is what gives the body life, what gives it the ability to move its limbs, to think, to feel, to love, to be.

When our Body Is in a Constant Process of Renewal, Why Do we Age?

Ok, so our body is in a constant process of renewal, so why does it age? The answer to this question is a complex one, and the main reason for the ageing is that the I, which holds the physical body together, can only concentrate for a certain amount of time on this process. As soon as the I releases itself from the physical body, the body starts to dissolve. It was the I that was in control of the cooperation of the various physical organs and cells, so the I is of paramount importance to the cohesion of the body. The ability of the I to maintain this cohesion is limited and after having reached its peak around the age of 30, the cohesion starts to relax and ageing sets in. At a certain point the I can no longer maintain the cohesion and it pulls out. The body dies.

So, the reason for the ageing is not in the physical body, but in the spiritual body. Also, as we evolve through our lives, we will need new bodies that correspond to the level of evolution our spirit has reached. It is always mind over matter, or spirit first. The physical bodies we inhabit are a direct reflection of our mental or evolutionary standard. For each life we live, our bodies evolve: we outlive certain tendencies, we outlive illnesses, we become milder, more humanitarian and more all-loving, so our bodies will be a reflection of this, our improved mental state. For that reason, we cannot have the same body all the time. Each time we reincarnate, we get a new body that reflects the level of evolution we have reached. We cannot have a modern man living in the coarse body of a Neanderthaler. For that reason, our bodies have to change a little bit for each life we live so that they accurately reflect the mental and evolutionary level we have reached.

Being outside the Body and Observing it from above

The simple fact that we are not our physical body has been illustrated to Else personally, because her husband once experienced being outside his body. When Erik was 10, he was playing with some friends at a farm, not far from where he lived. The boys were playing in the barn and had crawled up to the collar beams below the roof. From there they jumped into the hay below, even though they had been told not to do it. Well, boys will be boys and Erik jumped. After that he remembered nothing for a short time. After some minutes he observed, from a position high above the ground, that there was a procession of sorts carrying a lifeless boy into the wash house, where the body was placed on a large table. The people around the body were looking very distraught and at a loss about what to do. As Erik was observing this scene from his vantage point, he realized that the body was his. Oh dear, he thought, this is not so good. What will my mother say? I have to get back in there. He then performed what he describes as a dive aiming for the solar plexus. He then entered the body and opened his eyes. The people standing around him heaved a sigh of relief. He felt quite perplexed afterwards and walked slowly home, pulling his bicycle, trying to digest the episode. The experience had a profound impact on him, but he never told anybody until many years later when he finally understood what had happened. It left him with the unwavering conviction that he is not his physical body. But Erik's experience is far from exceptional. Many people have reported being outside their physical body, especially those who have had a near-death experience.

The Near-death Experience

Here we are just going to present a few accounts of near-death experiences. A near-death experience occurs when the physical body has stopped functioning and the body is declared clinically dead. When a body is clinically dead, the spirit has left. All three examples are from Raymond Moody's bestseller 'Life after Life' from 1975.

"It was about two years ago, and I had just turned nineteen. I was driving a friend of mine home in my car, and as I got to this particular intersection downtown, I stopped and looked both ways, but I didn´t see a thing coming. I pulled on out into the intersection and as I did I heard my friend yell at the top of his voice. When I looked I saw a blinding light, the headlights of a car that was speeding towards us. I heard this awful sound – the side of the car being crushed in – and there was just an instant during which I seemed to be going through a darkness, an enclosed space. It was very quick. Then, I was sort of floating about five feet above the street, about five yards away from the car, I´d say, and I heard the echo of the crash dying away. I saw people come running up and crowding around the car, and I saw my friend get out of the car, obviously in shock. I could see my own body in the wreckage among all those people and could see them trying to get me out. My legs were all twisted and there was blood all over the place". (Moody: "Life After Life", page 27).

Here is an account from a hospital:

"I remember being wheeled into the operating room and the next few hours were the critical period. During that time, I kept getting in and out of my physical body, and I could see it from directly above. But, while I did, I was still in a body – not a physical body, but something I can best describe as an energy pattern. If I had to put it into words, I would say that it was transparent, a spiritual as opposed to a material being... (Ibid, page 40)

And another one:

"I was out of my body looking at it from about ten yards away, but I was still thinking, just like in physical life. And where I was thinking was about at my normal bodily height. I wasn't in a body, as such. I could feel something, some kind of a – like a capsule, or something, like a clear form. I couldn't really see it; it was like it was transparent, but not really. It was like I was just there – an energy, maybe, sort of like just a little ball of energy... (Ibid, page 40).

The last two short accounts reflect the existence of an energy body (including consciousness, "I", and sense of self) as mentioned above. The persons could still see and think, and they felt that they existed in an energy body, but they still felt exactly the same as before.

These types of accounts from people who have been clinically dead and who, while their body was on the operating table, could observe what was going on in the room and sometimes in the corridor outside the room, have obviously puzzled the medical personnel. Again, within the belief that we are identical to our bodies, there is no room for such a phenomenon, but when we accept that we are not our body, but that we are primarily spiritual beings, it is not hard to understand that we can be outside the body and still be able to perceive and observe.

The Logic of Reincarnation

Those who are convinced that we only live once see nothing but injustice in the world. They see young children die before they reach the age of five, they see refugees drown trying to find a better life elsewhere, they see soldiers in their twenties die in war and they get very upset and say that the world is a very unjust place. And indeed, it would be, if we only lived once.

Where is the logic or justice if we only lived one life and one child is born to prosperous, caring parents and another child is born to neglectful, indifferent parents? If we really only lived once, what would the explanation be to that? Where would the justice be? Where would the logic be?

There would be neither explanation, justice nor logic in just living one miserable life and then that was it. What would the reason be behind such a short life? And why would another person live a successful, happy life and die at the age of 98? Is life just dished out randomly like food in a cheap canteen? Or could it be that the concept that we only live once is just a total misconception?

According to Martinus, the one-life theory has absolutely no foundation, not a logical one and certainly not a just one. If we really only lived one life, there would be no justice in the world. None. It would, as many people believe, all be governed by chance.

But we do not only live one life, and the death that a lot of people have a completely unfounded fear of is a huge illusion. There is no such death. What we perceive as death is nothing but a principle of maintenance, understood in the way that we discard the old and worn physical body and release our spirit from it. After a sojourn on the spiritual level, we reincarnate into a new and better body and continue our development in that. Death is the most natural process and it is not such a big deal as many people make it out to be. There is no death, just an exchange of bodies.

It makes no sense to live only once. What would the point be? If we only lived once, then why do we learn and practice things? All through life we reap experiences and wisdom, we grow mentally and morally, we become better at a lot of things, we become more humanitarian and compassionate. If all those aspects would only serve us in one life, then what a waste! Our life would be a complete waste of time. In nature we see that everything is used and recycled. This principle is visible for all to see, but if we only lived one life, then this principle would suddenly not be valid. Everything we had learned would just be wasted. Out of the window it goes. But that is fortunately not how things are. Everything we learn is saved and stored in our fate element and it will serve us in future lives. Nothing of what we have learned is wasted.

Once we realize that death is an illusion and that we do not only live once, then a whole new panorama is revealed before our eyes. We live an infinite number of lives, and if we died young in our last incarnation, then we may have a long life in the following.

This aspect means that what we did not achieve in one life, we can achieve in a later life. Today, we see so many people desperately struggling to achieve all their goals believing that if they do not succeed, then they will never experience the things they want. This is not an idea that is conducive to living a happy life, resting in peace in the now and appreciating what you have. Life then becomes a frantic struggle and the idea that we only live once makes everything stressful and pointless.

Today a lot of couples are trying to conceive a child and as this seems to have become increasingly difficult, a whole industry has arisen around assisted fertilization. The couples spend all their mental energy and large sums of money on the 'conceiving a child' project, and it often becomes exhausting and undermining for the relationship. Because they think they only live once, they think that, if they don't succeed, then they will NEVER experience what it is like to be a parent. They then feel that they have missed out on an important aspect of life and they become miserable and depressed. All for no reason. They have undoubtedly been parents in numerous previous incarnations and they will be in future lives. There is nothing definitive about 'not achieving what I want'. There is plenty of time ahead of us to make all our wishes come true. There really is no hurry and nothing to be stressed about. Eternity is our playground and we literally have all the time in the world.[2]

---

[2] The connection between the law of attraction and failure to conceive a child has not been well understood, but it is a fact that you cannot focus on the lack of something and at the same time attract it. Both Else and Maria have written books about the law of attraction and coming to grips with this law will be a huge help to all those desperate parents who want to conceive but cannot. It would help the process if they stopped focussing on the lack and focused on the simplicity of this natural process. Overthinking does not help here.

Nobody can understand his or her fate seen in a one-life perspective. The law of karma rules our fates and we reap as we sow.

What we have sown in one life can come back to us in a later life. We simply sow so much karma that there is not enough time in one life to get all of it back in the same incarnation. So, if we have sown darkness and misery for other living beings in a past life, then the ensuing karma will rule our fate in a following life. What we do to others, we eventually do to ourselves, so we ourselves are the masters of our fate.

The reaping of what we have once sown can stretch out over several future incarnations, and this is an important point to realize. Fate and karma will be the subject of the next book in this series – The Nutshell Series.

The universe is an extremely just place. There is a cosmic principle of responsibility at work and this means that every little thing we do will have consequences. If we do good deeds then they will return to us as good karma and if we do evil and unkind acts, then they will return to us as dark karma. In this life or in a future life. We are all at the steering wheel of our fate and everything we do comes back to us, sooner or later. It may take a long time for the karmic wave to come back to us, so a deed sown in one life can come back in a later life, but it will come back. The law of karma is relentless, but karma is not a punishment. It is a loving instruction nudging us in the right direction towards becoming real human beings.

The universe is so just, that *"even the hairs on your head are counted"*. This was pronounced by Jesus 2000 years ago, but how many of us realize this? Jesus also said: *"Put your sword back into its place; for all who take the sword will perish by the sword"*. (Matthew 26: 52). This is a direct reference to the law of karma: If you kill by the sword, you will be killed by the sword.

How could the world be a just place and how could the *"hairs on our head be counted"* if we only lived one life?

With the logic of reincarnation, a whole new perspective now lies before our wondering eyes. Our fates are levelled out over a series of lives and if one life is very miserable, we must understand that this life is just a single note in a whole song. A miserable life is not a final destination, but a single step on the road towards perfection. In later lives we will live in happiness and prosperity. We must all go through the same to become the same: Man, in the image and likeness of God. More about this later.

Where Do All the Souls Come from?

Some people refuse to believe in reincarnation because they say that it cannot be because the population of the earth is growing. As the number of people living here increases, then there would not be enough souls to inhabit the new bodies.

But that is a very limiting belief, indeed a belief that restricts life in the universe to one small planet: the earth. But life is not limited to this planet and life abounds everywhere. The whole universe is teeming with life and on innumerable planets there are humans just like us who are also on an evolutionary journey in bodies just like ours. We are not the only humanity alive in the universe and there are trillions and trillions of souls that are eager to reincarnate.

We belong to the same planet for a number of incarnations, indeed as long as our mentality is on wavelength with the mentality of the planet, which is also a living being. It lies beyond the boundaries of this small book to go further into this interesting topic but let us just say that our spirit can jump from one planet to another between incarnations according to eternal laws.[3]

There is no shortage of souls or spirits that can reincarnate on this planet. Indeed, Martinus says that the Earth has room for many more people than those who are here now.

The planet is a very rich and abundant place and it can cater for a much larger number of humans than those who are reincarnated here now. It will, of course, help when we reduce the number of livestock that also needs to be fed.

But as more and more people are shifting to a plant -based diet, it will not be a problem in the future.

The universe is a much more magical place than most people imagine.

Points to Ponder from Maria:

Re: Cell Renewal

When you look at a picture of yourself as a baby, don't you ever think 'Wow, how was that possibly ever me?' Or you flick through an old photo album (or phone these days!) and see yourself at different ages and think 'how different I look now!'... the fact is, we are constantly reincarnating not only our physical bodies but also our spiritual ones. I'm 60 as I write

---

[3] You can read more about this interesting aspect in Else's book: The Beginning Is Near, where she explains how the earth, which is a living being, attracts all the living beings that are reincarnated here. This process follows eternal laws and it is fascinating.

this, and I know for a fact I am not the same person I was when I was 20. How could I possibly be? We are all constantly learning, growing, developing and evolving emotionally and spiritually with every passing moment.

Think back on your life at the moment and consider the different stages of your younger you. How much wiser are you now? How much more emotionally mature? Almost all of us can immediately see that we have changed. Else explains this by showing us 3 photos of Martinus, but I also remember reading about this concept by Dr Wayne Dyer in his book "Wishes Fulfilled".

In it he says: 'Consider how many bodies you've occupied since birth. Who is the I that continues to leave one body behind and then enter another? You know for certain that you – the person that you call I, the one attempting to figure out who you are – started out in a little baby body weighing somewhere between five and ten pounds. The I that is you fully entered and occupied that little baby body. Gradually you began to discard that baby body and move into a small toddler body that crawled, then walked, then ran, and took on an entirely new appearance. Your two-year old self would find it difficult to recognize the baby body that you'd now completely abandoned.'

From this Dyer concludes (and I paraphrase here) that you are obviously not your body, because it changes all the time. He says that though he can well remember what his 20-year-old body looked like, was capable of, etc., that body as it once was has completely vanished from existence. It is an illusion, gone from this physical world, as is every body we all have occupied in our lifetime. And that it is absolutely clear that you are not your body. When you really think about this, it makes sense doesn't it? Our one constant I is all that is constant in that it cannot cease to be. It can only grow and evolve.

So, we are constantly reincarnating in each life! When you throw into the mix what we now know about cell regeneration, and that all our cells replicate, and we make new ones all the time, to the point that every few years we have a completely new set of cells, how can we possibly say that we don't believe in reincarnation?

If this isn't enough to convince you, then taking a look at the vast body of work that has been done on Near Death Experiences (NDEs) and Out of Body Experiences (OBEs) might just tip the balance. If we were not pure spirit, how could anyone die, but witness themselves from above, lying dead below, then come back and tell everyone what went on? So many cases have validated the phenomenon of OBEs & NDEs that it becomes very difficult to discount them as illusions or dreams or plain crazy!

One of the most powerfully convincing stories of an NDE I've read (and I've read a LOT) is "Proof of Heaven", by Dr Eben Alexander. He is a worldwide authority on developing advanced neurosurgical technology for complex disorders of the brain. Now if anyone can argue the case for whether NDEs are a product of some or other kind of brain function or malfunction, it's Dr Alexander. Prior to his own NDE, he held the belief that NDEs were brain-based illusions. His own experience was to radically change his perspective. His NDE in 2008 left him convinced beyond a shadow of a doubt, that the brain does not house our consciousness. He meticulously researched his own medical records after his recovery, and it was clear that he had been brain dead. But, he explains in his book, he was totally alive. He was more alive and everything was more real than anything he had ever experienced. His book is also well worth reading to get the whole story, and he has since written two more.

Once you start delving into these kinds of books, the case for reincarnation becomes just too strong to ignore. There is too much logic to it. Too much that makes sense. Else briefly touches on the logic of reincarnation and again, everything she wrote in Death Is An Illusion just made sense to me. It made too much sense to reject it. It worked to explain everything that I had sought to understand for so many years. Yes! This is it! I hope that when you give these concepts deep thought yourself, light bulbs will start popping all over the place for you too. Karmic debt is of course a huge part of the whole process, and we have such a lot to share about that that it will become the second book in the Nutshell Series.

But to consider your own 'current life' ongoing reincarnation process, find 3 pictures of yourself – one when you were a baby, one when you were perhaps in your early teens, and one of yourself now, and compare them. Just let yourself be open to the reality of what has happened... of course we all grow and develop and change, but we never really stop to *think* about it... the physical body we 'were' no longer exists. We're here now in a different body from the one we came into the world with. Isn't it fascinating to think about this?

Re: The Logic of Reincarnation

I also consider this to be deeply illuminating in helping us to understand the so-called injustices of the world, both today and historically. That is not to say that we needn't or shouldn't feel concern, pity, or try to help those who are suffering. To do so shows our compassion and that is always going to be a good thing for our soul. However, when you look at injustice from the bigger picture of the soul's evolving journey though countless lives, where it has to learn compassion by suffering, that it has to pay back karmic debt in the process, that everyone has suffered, or will have to suffer equally, at some point or other, then the whole picture starts to make a lot more sense that believing we live just once, and that's that. As Else has pointed out, where would be the justice, the fairness, the sense – in living just one life? Why should one person be born healthy, beautiful, wealthy, whilst another is born deformed, ugly and in poverty? It just makes no sense whatsoever. There has to be another plan. And I believe Martinus has given us the logic to understand that divine plan. What is your gut feeling on this? Consider it and let it percolate for a while in your mind if you're still not sure. Deep down, there is a part of you that knows the truth of who we truly are, but it's been buried for so long, it can take some time to let that truth re-emerge.

Re: Where Do all the Souls Come from?
I wondered about this too, and I also wondered why, with the dawn of birth control and the fact that women are having fewer children now than ever, why the population continues to grow. The answer, according a report by Worldwatch Institute, is due to two factors:

"The seeming contradiction between smaller-than-ever families and near-record births is easily explained. The number of women of childbearing age keeps growing and global life expectancy at birth continues to rise. These two trends explain why population continues growing despite declines in family size. There were 1.7 billion women aged 15 to 49 in late 2007, compared with 856 million in 1970. The average human being born today can expect to live 67 years, a full decade longer than the average new-born could expect in 1970."

So that answered my question. However, much more fascinating to me was the idea that there are souls on other planets who are (to quote Else) 'Queuing up to get here!' Wow! Now I've always thought that we cannot be alone in the universe… when you consider the vastness of the galaxy, and the planets and space we know of, never mind those we don't yet know of because of our limited scientific capacity to expand that knowledge, isn't it rather arrogant and naïve of us to think that we are the only humans alive in the universe? Yet our planet is marvellously unique in what it can offer the soul in search of evolution. Doesn't that make you appreciate this rare earth we inhabit all the more?

Also interesting to me was the idea that the earth has room for 'many more people than those who are here now'. This gave me pause when I first heard of it because we are constantly being reminded of how the world is over-populated, global warming and climate change are happening and our world is on the brink of peril and of perishing. But it's just not true. The earth will never perish because much bigger forces than we can possibly imagine are at play.

I hasten to add here however that this is not to say we should disrespect our amazing planet. Absolutely not. We should, and Else and I do as much as is possible in our daily lives to play our part, i.e., recycling, not wasting food, water, resources, respecting the environment etc. I believe that is ALL our duty to the earth.

But where are all these new souls going to fit? Which brings us to livestock, and I promise not to beat you over the head now with the vegetarian/vegan stick, but just consider these facts because they have a huge impact on the planet, the environment, the atmosphere, and indeed, the available space on our planet - and that's leaving out the moral implications!

So…here's the scoop from an article published in 2012 by www.smithsonian.com

(link: https://www.smithsonianmag.com/travel/is-the-livestock-industry-destroying-the-planet-11308007/)

"The global scope of the livestock issue is huge. A 212-page online report published by the United Nations Food and Agriculture Organization says 26 percent of the earth's terrestrial surface is used for livestock grazing. One-third of the planet's arable land is occupied by livestock feed crop cultivation. Seventy percent of Brazil's deforested land is used as pasture, with feed crop cultivation occupying much of the remainder. And in Botswana, the livestock industry consumes 23 percent of all water used. Globally, 18 percent of greenhouse gas emissions can be attributed to the livestock industry—more than is produced by transportation-related sources. And in the United States, livestock production is responsible for 55 percent of erosion, 37 percent of all applied pesticides and 50 percent of antibiotics consumed, while the animals themselves directly consume 95 percent of our oat production and 80 percent of our corn, according to the Sierra Club."

And an article from Our World in Data in 2017 states that *'…the world population uses approximately 50 percent of total habitable land for agriculture."*

(Link: https://ourworldindata.org/agricultural-land-by-global-diets)

And one final piece I want to share with you is this:

'According to calculations of the United Nations Environment Programme, the calories that are lost by feeding cereals to animals, instead of using them directly as human food, could theoretically feed an extra 3.5 billion people.'

(Link: https://www.globalagriculture.org/report-topics/meat-and-animal-feed.html)

The point of considering all this is to show that the biggest chunk of habitable earth is used to feed and house livestock, which are then slaughtered for food. Coming back to the point of the world having room for plenty more people, if we stopped slaughtering animals and instead starting living on a plant-based diet, there certainly would be a lot more room for growing more people! And we could (theoretically) feed an extra 3.5 billion people! Food for thought, isn't it?

But, as Else points out, more and more people are shifting to a plant-based diet; the slow but definite global shift in consciousness has already begun.

4. The Spiritual World

Where Does the Spirit Go when it Leaves the Physical Body?

So, we have established that it is the spirit package with consciousness and sense of self or I that survives the death of the physical body. The spirit is of an electrical nature and it provides the energy that makes it possible for the physical body to be alive and move its limbs.

We now say that the spirit has left the physical body, which consequently has become a corpse. We are extremely curious to know what happens to the spirit. Where does it go? What is it up to?

Everything is Vibration

In order to answer that question, we must again repeat that the spirit is a magnetic field, and like all other energetic entities, it has a specific wavelength that it operates on. The wavelength varies from one magnetic field to the other. Everything is vibration and the specific wavelength of any magnetic field is defined by a number of factors. The wavelength of the magnetic field of the spirit is defined by the vibration of the type of thoughts it thinks. Each thought we think has a specific vibration and a whole bunch of thoughts form a specific wavelength.

A consciousness holding a lot of thoughts of a humanitarian and all-loving nature will operate on a wavelength that is different from that of a consciousness that holds a lot of thoughts of revenge and hatred. The wavelength of any spirit is defined by the vibration and quality of the thought matter that is predominant in its consciousness. It is so because thoughts are electrical currents, and because the contents of the various thoughts are different, then so is their vibration. Everything is vibration, and the vibration defines the wavelength. The vibration of a loving thought will be different from the vibration of a hateful thought. The conjunction of a lot of hateful thoughts, indeed a whole consciousness full of them, will constitute a specific wavelength. A consciousness full of loving and humanitarian thoughts will have a totally different vibration and consequently its wavelength will be different from that of the hateful consciousness.

Depending on its wavelength the spirit package will be attracted to a place in the spiritual world that has a similar wavelength to its own, because like attracts like as decreed by the law of attraction.

The spiritual world is a world consisting of invisible spiritual matter or thought matter. The thought matter is energy. As mentioned, Martinus calls this type of matter ray-formed matter. The spiritual world is arranged through wavelengths. It is a world organized in a hierarchical manner according to the vibration of the various wavelengths. The spiritual world is everywhere in 'empty space', but for those of us who at our present stage belong to the earth, our spiritual world will be in the aura of the earth. Like all other living beings, the earth has an aura, which holds its consciousness, spirit or I, and our destination in the spiritual world will be a 'place' in the aura of the earth.

Aura of the earth as it would look if it were symmetrical (source ESA)

The Law of Attraction

The law of attraction decrees that similar wavelengths attract each other and that dissimilar wavelengths repel each other. The law of attraction is the most important natural law at work in the universe because it decides the movement of all ray-formed matter.

This means that the wavelength of the particular spirit that has now left the physical body will automatically be attracted to a wavelength in the spiritual world that corresponds to its own. This attraction of the spirit to a specific wavelength will be felt by the spirit like a very fast movement through space. This is what is felt by many near-death 'experiencers' as a superfast passage through a tunnel or narrow space. Our being placed in the spiritual world is ruled by the law of attraction and we can feel this movement at lightspeed through space as a superfast flight through a narrow space. Our destination is a wavelength that corresponds to our own.

If you are a very loving person, your spirit will be attracted, via its wavelength, to a place in the spiritual world where loving thoughts prevail. Birds of a feather flock together, and that means that a loving spirit will go to a wavelength where there are other loving spirits. This means that the contents of your consciousness, meaning the overall quality of your mentality and the type of thoughts that predominate your way of thinking, will decide where you go in the spiritual world. It is quite simple really. The law of attraction will pull you to where your like-minded spirits dwell.

In the case of a loving person who is always ready to lend a helping hand, who cares for others, who does not kill, maim and molest others, s/he will go to a wavelength where thoughts of a similar kind as those that predominate her/ his consciousness dwell. The loving wavelength will be inhabited by other loving beings and it will be a very pleasant place to be.

A person who all his life has run around hating other people, who has been practicing egoism, greed, jealousy, envy, stealing, murder or terrorism, will also go to a wavelength that corresponds to that type of thinking. Here the person / spirit will meet others with the same type of mind-set, and it will be a less pleasant place to be.

Your mental sphere, the type of person you are, the kind of thoughts you feed into your consciousness define your wavelength. And your wavelength defines where you go when you pass over. This happens quite automatically due to the workings of the law of attraction.

In the spiritual world there are many destinations. There are as many destinations as there are types of consciousness. This is actually what Jesus refers to when he says, *"In my Father's house there are many mansions"*.

So, when your spirit leaves your physical body, it enters the spiritual world on a wavelength that corresponds to its own. That is the short answer.

In this connection it may be good to know, that we are always 'placed' according to the wavelength of the most developed and loving part of our psyche. We all have sides to our psyche that are quite well developed, and we also have sides that may be more primitive and not so 'pretty'. It is the most developed aspects of our psyche or mentality that decide where we go.

Aspects of the Spiritual World

In the spiritual world things work differently from here on the physical plane. The spiritual world is a light world of thoughts or ray-formed matter and it offers no resistance.

In the spiritual world, you live in your spiritual body, in your energy field. It is who you really are, so your sense of self is no different from when you still had your physical body. You are simply the same person, only lighter. Because the spiritual world is a light world of energy, there is no ground to step on. The absence of a firm surface to stand on is something that we have to get used to. Also, the day is not divided by meals, because there is no need to eat. There is no need to sleep either. In the spiritual world you are constantly alert and ready to explore this world.

When you pass over, you will be met by your spiritual guides or guardian angels that are there to help you adjust to this level of existence. Help is always at hand. Should you feel lost, just ask for help and it will come. Your guardian angels will rush in to assist you.

You will most certainly be met by family members who have passed before you and who are eager to welcome you back into spirit and spend time with you again. It will be a time of happy reunions.

But there are many other aspects. In the physical world it is hard to make things. First, we have an idea (a construction in thought or ray-formed matter) and then we make a drawing based on the idea of the thing we want to create. Then we must go and get materials for our creation and then we must spend time putting them together. This may take skills and talents, so it is not that easy. In order to become good at creating things, we need to practice a lot, but then we may improve in our skills. After a lot of practicing, we can end up being quite good at producing a specific creation.

In the spiritual world things are a lot easier because of the lack of resistance of that world. It is a light world of thoughts and that means that when you think of something, that thing will materialize immediately before your eyes. If you think of a car, it will at once materialize before your eyes in all its glory. When you think of a person that you have known and who is in the spiritual world, that person will stand before you in the blink of an eye. You can then have a pleasant conversation via telepathy, as no words are necessary in that world.

In the spiritual world you can live the life of your dreams. If you, in your physical life, were very interested in learning and wisdom, you will live in a world of scholars and intellectual pastimes. You may even get access to the huge spiritual library, sometimes referred to as the Akashic records, where all wisdom is kept. If you were an artist, you will live in a world of art and beautiful creations, and if you were a cook, you will be able to create wonderful dishes by just thinking of them. It is indeed a paradisiacal world.

How to Improve your Destination in the Spiritual World

It is useful to know that your destination in the spiritual world is defined by your interests and thoughts on the physical plane. It is useful because then you can prepare for where you go after death while you are still in a physical body. You can do so by working to improve your mix of thoughts. If you tend to be judgemental towards other people, then you can practice being less so. You can practice forgiving others and sending love to them. You can practice not being irritated and worried, you can practice being kind and loving. The more you focus on positive aspects of life, the more you help others, the more you abstain from hurting and killing (also animals), the better will your place be in the afterlife. It ´pays´ to be positive, good, honest and loving. If you do not know that already, you will know on the other side. The good news is that you can start practicing right away and thus prepare a better ´seat´ for yourself on the other side.

Time and Eternity

Another aspect of the spiritual world is that there is no time. Everything happens in an eternal now. There is no tomorrow and no yesterday, and the concept of time has no meaning whatsoever. A thousand years is like one second and one second is like a thousand years.

This aspect has been confirmed by several near-death ´experiencers´.

"My sense of time was way off. Time didn´t mean anything. It seemed like time had no meaning". Kenneth Ring: "Life at Death", page 97.

"(What was your sense of time like when you were in this state?) Very bad. I really have no idea of how long this went on. Sometimes, when I think about it, it seems like it was forever...." Kenneth Ring: "Life at Death", page 97.

The aspect of being outside time is also referred to by Jesus: "But do not ignore this one fact, beloved, that with the Lord one day is as a thousand years, and a thousand years as one day" (2 Pet, 3,8).

There are many other interesting aspects of the spiritual plane and we shall look at them in the final chapter of this book.

How Long Are We Discarnate?

We now have our spirit / consciousness / I placed in the spiritual world on a wavelength that corresponds to the wavelength that our own psyche or mentality operates on. How long do we stay there?

The length of our stay in the spiritual world depends a lot on the life we lived before we died. If we lived a long life and died of old age, then our stay will be approximately the same as the time we lived on Earth. If we lived to be a 100, then we will stay on the spiritual plane for around 100 years. As there is no concept of time on the spiritual plane, we will not feel the years. We will feel our stay as a wonderful long holiday in the surroundings of our liking. We will also go and visit some of the many realms there, so it will be a pleasant and interesting stay. We shall look at some of the other realms in the final chapter.

If we died young, say in an accident, then our stay on the spiritual plane will be much shorter. We will maybe be eager to return to the physical plane because our life there was cut short, so we may return after only a few years. It depends on our own wishes and on our spiritual guides.

Soldiers, who die in war, will typically reincarnate after about 7 years. Most soldiers also die young, so their life was cut short too, and they will want to go back to the earth quickly to get on with their development.

But why, when the spiritual plane is such a nice place, does anyone want to go back to the earth plane? The physical plane is full of resistance and hardship, a lot of suffering takes place there, so why bother? Why not stay in paradise?

Our Journey of Evolution

Well, that option is not really possible. It is not possible, because we are all on a journey. A very long journey indeed. This journey started in the mineral kingdom and via the plant and animal kingdoms we have now reached the human kingdom. The evolution of life on Earth is something that each and every one of us has undertaken.

The evolution of humankind is a journey that each and every one of us has undertaken

We were the plant that was growing in the jungle, we were the antelope that ran around on the grasslands, we were the soldier in the Roman army, we participated in the French revolution and we were the victims of the bombings during WW2. The whole evolution of life on earth has been lived through by each and every one of us personally. It is our spirit or I that has reincarnated into all the individual plants, animals and people who have inhabited the earth. In tune with the advances we made in each life, our consciousness evolved, and our bodies had to follow suit. The primitive mentality gave rise to a primitive human being and a more advanced mentality gave rise to a more advanced human being. It is always mind over matter or the mentality that decides the physical manifestation. Our physical bodies will always be a manifestation in physical matter of our mental level of evolution.

So, when we talk about our ancestors, they were us. It was not somebody else who lived before us. It was us. Through reincarnation each of us has lived through the whole of human evolution. And we are not home free yet. We still have some distance to go before we reach our final destination. And what is our final destination? Well, our final destination is to become ´Man in the image and likeness of God´.

Man, in the Image and Likeness of God

What does that mean? What is ´man in the image and likeness of God´? A man or woman in the image and likeness of God is a person who loves all other beings and lives to serve others. It is a person who can no longer harbour egoism, jealousy or envy, who cannot hate, main, kill or seek revenge. It is a person who can no longer eat the flesh of other living beings and it is a person who emanates peace, friendship and love towards everybody. Such a person can no longer become irritated or angry, cannot express intolerance or disdain towards others, such a person is happier to give than to take, is absolutely not greedy and does not want power. S/he forgives everybody who has wronged them because s/he knows that they did not know what they were doing. They did not know what they were doing because they had not yet accumulated enough wisdom in their fate element to be wise enough to know what they were doing. S/he lives in gratitude for all things in life and knows that only humility will open the gates to wisdom. Jesus was an example of a man in the image and likeness of God.

In this connection it is important to understand that not everybody stands on the same level of evolution. Some have begun their journey of evolution earlier than others, so they have progressed further than others. This is easy to see when we look at the population of the planet today. Some are very aggressive and warlike. They find it quite OK to go out and kill others and will even kill themselves in terrorist attacks if they are hateful enough. They have no consideration for the wellbeing of others and they act only to make themselves more powerful and rich. Money and power is their mantra and they will ruthlessly eliminate anybody who stands in their way.

At the other end of the scale we have the very compassionate and all-loving person. S/he works only to be of service to others and wants to help wherever it is possible. Such a person cares about the wellbeing of others and will work tirelessly to create peace and harmony on the planet. They will rather give than take, they cannot hurt, harm or kill and live only on a plant-based diet.

In between these two extremes we find the population of the planet with a wide range of qualities. Some are quite good, some are really bad, some are very good, some are quite bad and so on. We all have different levels of development of our good and bad sides, but we are all moving in the direction of becoming ´man in the image and likeness of God´. The Man in the image and likeness of God is a perfect human being. This means that we are all on our way towards perfection. One day each and every one of us will become a perfect human being that can only emanate love, understanding, tolerance and peace. However, we are not there yet, but the perfect stage for all humans is in the process of being created. Some have come a long way towards perfection, some have not come so far and some still have a long way to go. But we are all on our way and everybody will reach the goal sooner or later.

It is only on the physical plane that we can progress towards perfection. Why is that so? It is so because on the spiritual plane there is no resistance, so it is not a place where we can learn from our mistakes. The spiritual plane is a place to rest, not to work. We cannot progress in our evolution on the spiritual plane, we can only relax and enjoy life there. And while we are there, having a five-star experience, we know that we, sooner or later, will have to go back to the physical plane to get on with our development. We can only progress and add experience, knowledge, wisdom, talents and compassion to our fate element through a life in physical matter. The physical plane offers enough resistance to make us learn from our mistakes. As all our knowledge, harvested during a lifetime, is stored in our fate element, it is clear that we progress for each life we live, and, in this way, it is also clear that we are all moving towards the perfect stage, or becoming ´man in the image and likeness of God´.

So, after some time on the spiritual plane, where we have enjoyed a good rest, we know that it is time to get back onto the physical level and get on with our development. There is nothing else to do, we MUST go back. If we do not, our development will be halted, and it is not in our own best interest.

But how do we get back onto the physical plane? How do we get our spirit back into a new physical body? We do that during the process of reincarnation.

Points to Ponder from Maria:

Re: The Spiritual World

I think this section once again hammers home the point that our thoughts are all-important. Thoughts, as Else states, are electrical currents that attract similar currents back to them, so here on earth it is vital to your health and wellbeing that you fill your mind with loving, life-affirming thoughts. But of course it doesn't end with this life, as we hope this book is making very clear. Your thoughts, your vibrational resonance, determine what happens to you when you pass over. I also found it fascinating that the spiritual world is everywhere in 'empty space'... effectively, it is in the earth's aura. Could this in fact be what we think of as 'Heaven'? What an interesting thought!

Consider the Law of Attraction again, even though we've mentioned it many times before. You are always going to be attracting that which you focus on and give your thought energy to. Make those thoughts the best, most loving ones possible.

Else also points out that a person who is filled with hate will be attracted to a wavelength that corresponds to that type of thinking. I believe this is the real hell that people fear. Hell is indeed of your own making. Never wish anyone to perish in hell for that is a negative vibe for you to carry. When you understand the Law of Attraction at the deep level within, you will know that those who commit evil acts have already condemned themselves to 'hell'. By the same token of this deep understanding, you will also come to know and believe that if you yourself have suffered terrible trauma or evil, it is your karmic payback for something you did to someone else in a previous life.

This may seem like a hard pill to swallow but if you really think about it and circle back to the logic of the evolutionary soul cycle, does it not make sense to you? When I came to really understand this concept it had a profound impact on my thinking. Whilst I can, and do, of course have sympathy for anyone suffering, I always think that for some karmic reason this has happened to him or her, or to myself, to help us grow our own compassion. Martinus teaches us that we cannot learn compassion without suffering ourselves and when you really think about it, once again it makes perfect sense. Every one of us has suffered horrible fates and done terrible things to other human beings and animals in our journey to then learning compassion via our own suffering and thus, becoming more evolved human beings ourselves.

Re: Aspects of the Spiritual World

Have you ever wondered about how different life might be in the spiritual realm? I know I've often thought about it. Would we need sleep? Would we need food? But of course, it makes sense that if we are purely spirit beings, we wouldn't need either. We are light energy, and there is no more pain, even if we have suffered a horrible disease and 'died' because of it. And it makes perfect sense that we wouldn't need food if we don't have a physical body. Food is only necessary to sustain life on the physical plane. And isn't it a lovely thought that you can participate in activities that brought you joy on earth? Why would all that suddenly stop? Everything would be easier. Isn't this what Heaven really is? What we find in the spiritual realm is what we have found joy in here, or what we have longed to have. What would your Heaven look like?

Re: Time and Eternity

Having read a lot of books about OBEs and NDEs, and having been a hypnotherapist for many years, I'm well aware of the concept that time can be expanded. It is very simple to suggest to a client under hypnosis that 4 minutes seems like 15. I've done it many times. Time as we know it is only applicable on this physical plane. We have day and night, in a span of 24 hours as the earth revolves around itself, and time helps us organize our lives. But in the spiritual realm, there is no need for such organization. Time is endless. We can never run out of it! If you can stretch your imagination to believe that there is a realm where time as we understand it simply does not exist, can you grasp just a tiny seed of what that could be like? I couldn't for a long time but with constantly reading and exploring the concept, I eventually 'got' it.

I had a discussion once with a guy who was trying to sell me a funeral plan. We started talking about the galaxy. He was an atheist, and he mentioned the sheer size of the known galaxy. He scoffed at the idea that God could create all this in 7 days. I pointed out that of course He could not create it in our version of 7 days of 'reality', but in the zone of timelessness where God is, 7 days can be expanded or compressed and He could have created the world in an instant! We humans always need to frame things in a way that makes sense to us!

Re: How Long Are We Discarnate?

This is an interesting one and I had a question for Else, when I read that we would be discarnate roughly as long as we had been on the physical plane. So, what of the young child who dies, leaving grief-stricken parents – is it possible that the child would reincarnate to the same parents? Else said that it is possible, and it has been reported to happen. She told me a story about a couple who had lost a 4-year-old son. The parents were, of course, devastated, but after a few years they had a new son. When he was old enough to speak, he would reveal knowledge that he could not have achieved in his 3 years in the family. He would point to a high cupboard and say to his parents: please give me the yellow toys that I had the last time I was here with you, they are in that cupboard, don't you remember? Statements like that and many other incidences convinced the parents that the same son had returned to them. Needless to say, they were overjoyed and also baffled, because at the time nobody could explain how this could happen.

Re: Man, in the Image and Likeness of God

Else points out that such a person forgives everybody who has wronged them, because he or she (the offender) did not know what they were doing, because they had not yet accumulated enough wisdom in their fate element to be wise enough to know what they were doing. I think it's important to point out here that this does not mean we must accept such wrongdoing or downright evil acts. We must always strive to do what we can to prevent harm and suffering – by being better people ourselves, and by helping others who are less fortunate or who are in circumstances where they need help to be freed from any kind of abuse.

5. The Process of Reincarnation

So, how do we get our spirit package back into a physical body? This process has been explained meticulously by Martinus.

Again, as in the case of how we are placed in the spiritual realms when we pass over, the process of reincarnation into a new physical body is determined by the law of attraction. It is the wavelength of our spirit that decides where we go, because like wavelengths attract like wavelengths.

It happens like this: In the spiritual world there are various realms, and we shall look at those later, but here we can state that all reincarnation takes place from the realm or kingdom of bliss, as Martinus calls it.

Once our spirit reaches the kingdom of bliss it has spent a considerable time on the spiritual plane and it is mentally ready to go back to the physical level to get on with its development. It wants to reincarnate. It is eager to go back into a physical body and recommence a life in physical matter.

In its spiritual body, our I emanates a specific wavelength, defined by the person it has become through its journey, by the type of thoughts it thinks and how far it has evolved towards becoming an all-loving being.

The Intercourse or Act of Copulation

We all know that the act that produces a baby is intercourse. We know that it is a highly desirable activity and one that a lot of us are eager to participate in. But do we also know why the act can be so incredibly satisfying, arguably the most physically satisfying activity we can undertake here on the physical plane? Not everybody knows that around the act of intercourse there is an important spiritual aura or area. When two people are attracted to each other and fall in love, they get in contact with the very spirit of God, by Martinus referred to as The Highest Fire. When we are in love, the highest fire rushes through our whole being and we feel electrified and elated. Being in love is better than anything. And it is better than anything because during that phase we are in contact with the highest fire or the very spirit of God. It is as close to the divine level as we can come here at this stage of evolution. No wonder we are all quite interested in having sex.

Sexuality constitutes the core of the divine principle of creation and that is why it is so powerful. When we are under its spell, we are eager to feel the incredible rush of being lifted above the trivial earthly plane and up to a place where we can feel closer to the divine. The act of intercourse has been adorned with this divine aura so that we will gladly engage in sex. This is so for various reasons, the main one being that there are many spirits on the spiritual plane that are eager to reincarnate, and they can only do that on the wings of the all-pervasive power of the sexual principle. And no, having sex is not a sin. Whoever had that idea is completely ignorant about this sublime activity.

Because of the power of the sexual principle, we have a large number of couples engaged in the activity of making love on the physical plane. During the act, each of those couples emanates a specific joint wavelength. Because of their love-making an aura of divine presence has been added to their normal wavelength due to the power of the highest fire.

The Meaning of Orgasm

Under normal conditions physical beings cannot reach a wavelength high and fine enough to reach a spirit seeking reincarnation from the spiritual level. But during intercourse and especially during orgasm, the physical beings reach a very fine and high vibration. This high and fine vibration is built up gradually during the intercourse and it culminates in the orgasm. During orgasm the beings emit a vibration that is high and strong enough to reach a discarnate spirit on the spiritual level. This spiritual being will then be attracted to a specific lovemaking couple, who will then become its new parents. The wavelengths of the spiritual being seeking reincarnation and the lovemaking couple have to have enough similarities in order to be able to attract each other. For that reason, the spirit will be attracted to parents of his own species that match his own mental and evolutionary level to a large degree. The law of attraction sees to it that the spirit and the parents fit on a series of parameters and it is the ´job´ of the orgasm to bring the vibration of the physical couple up to a lever high enough to reach a discarnate being seeking reincarnation on the spiritual plane.

This is the ideal scenario. But it is a well-known fact that fertilization can also take place in cases of rape or artificial insemination. Let us just briefly have a look at those two aspects.

Martinus says that the most important criterion for fertilization to take place is that the egg and the sperm cell unite. In the sperm cell there is a large amount of spiritual energy, enough for it to be able, in certain cases, to attract a spiritual being on its own.

In cases of rape it is fortunately so that the likelihood of conception is smaller than during lovemaking between willing partners, because the woman is being forced and is doing what she can to dissociate herself from the act. Unfortunately conception can still take place during rape because the primary criterion has been fulfilled.

Fertilization can even take place through artificial insemination, where there is no act of lovemaking at all. Again, this is possible because the principal criterion of the two cells uniting can be fulfilled. And, even after freezing, the sperm cell will hold enough spiritual attraction power to attract a discarnate being. However, Martinus points out that a child conceived through artificial insemination will be born with a deficit: he or she will have difficulties conceiving and will have a limited ability to produce offspring. This is due to the fact that an important spiritual element is lacking in the process: the highest fire. The highest fire is conducive to fertilization taking place in the optimal way.

Interestingly, this aspect has been confirmed by a study made by a research team from the National Hospital Department of Growth and Reproduction (Rigshospitalet, Copenhagen) and the University of Southern Denmark. The research team examined the sperm quality in a group of 1925 conscripts, of which 47 were conceived with some kind of medical help. In these 47 young men the sperm count was significantly lower than in the rest. On average, they had a sperm concentration (number of sperm cells per milliliter of semen) which was 46% lower than the rest of the group, and their sperm count (amount of sperm in a single dose of semen) was 45 % lower. Their testicles were also slightly smaller than those of the other conscripts. The young men who had been conceived artificially were simply not as fertile as those who had been conceived in the normal way.

Do we choose our parents?

So, do we choose our new parents? Yes and no. It is not as if we are handed a catalogue of potential parents and can choose from that. But we choose our parents on the basis of the person we have become, because like wavelengths attract like wavelengths. Our vibration and wavelength define who will become our next parents, simply because we will be attracted to a love-making couple whose joint wavelength has a certain match to our own. This means that we will be born to parents who 'resemble' us in certain aspects, such as morals, tendencies, intelligence, interests, talents etc. It is, as mentioned, the law of attraction that is at work here, so the attraction to the 'right' parents happens automatically due to the attraction identical wavelengths have on each other.

Symbol no. 34

We are going to look at one of Martinus' symbols, no. 34, that illustrates what happens during conception. The three round figures with the triangles in the middle symbolise living beings, in this case a man, a woman and a discarnate being ready for reincarnation. The orange circle at the bottom, left hand corner symbolizes that of the man of the sexual act, the orange circle at the right symbolizes the woman of the act and the indigo coloured circle at the top symbolizes the discarnate spirit seeking reincarnation. The large yellow field that goes out from each of the sexual partners symbolizes their vibration during the act of intercourse. The grey-yellow area symbolizes that contact has been made between a discarnate being and the two physical beings due to their similarity in vibration. During the culmination of the act of copulation, symbolized by the flames between the two partners, some tread-like figures go out from the lovers and reach up to the discarnate being, where they envelop that being and pull him / her in towards the fertilized egg in the womb. This can be seen on the symbol via the treads circling the female on the right of the symbol.

Once the discarnate being has 'joined the party' or been pulled in, the creation of a new physical being begins.

Here you can see the symbol together with the obligatory explanation from the Martinus Institute.

A Summary Explanation of Symbol No. 34 - The Act of Copulation or God's Spirit in the Darkness (obligatory official explanation of the Martinus Institute)

THE SYMBOL SYMBOLISES THE MAJOR PRINCIPLES THAT WORK TOGETHER IN THE ACT OF COPULATION. MARTINUS DESCRIBES HOW THE SPIRIT OF GOD DIRECTLY PERVADING ALL LIVING BEINGS IS THE VERY HIGHEST PRINCIPLE OF THE EXPERIENCE OF LIFE. THE BEINGS MUST GO THROUGH DARKNESS IN ORDER TO GAIN THE ABILITY TO PERSONALLY EXPERIENCE KNOWLEDGE, BEAUTY, LOVE AND BLISS. BUT NO BEING IS LEFT ALONE DURING THIS EXPERIENCE OF DARKNESS. THROUGH BUILT-IN SPECIAL ORGANS IN THE ORGANISM IT HAS THE POSSIBILITY TO EXPERIENCE TANGIBLY IN THE MIDDLE OF DARKNESS A RAY OF LIGHT FROM GOD'S ETERNAL OCEAN OF

LIGHT OR ABUNDANCE OF LOVE. THIS DIVINE RAY FROM GOD'S
ETERNAL OCEAN OF LIGHT IS THE BEINGS' HIGHEST LEADING
AND GUIDING FORCE IN THEIR PRIMITIVE STATE AND THEIR

© Martinus Idealfond 1994   Reg. 34

EXPERIENCE OF DARKNESS. HERE THEY EXPERIENCE IN
GLIMPSES LIFE'S VERY HIGHEST FEELING OF PLEASURE IN THE
FORM OF THE "HIGHEST FIRE" IN THE ACT OF COPULATION. THE
ACT OF COPULATION IS A STIMULUS THAT PROMOTES ZEST FOR
LIFE AT THE SAME TIME AS IT PROVIDES THE ORGANIC
OPPORTUNITY FOR THE BEINGS TO BE BORN ANEW IN PHYSICAL
MATTER.

THE MAIN DETAILS OF THE SYMBOL:

- THE ROUND FIGURE AT THE BOTTOM LEFT SYMBOLISES A MALE BEING, AND THE FIGURE AT THE BOTTOM RIGHT SYMBOLISES A FEMALE BEING.
- THE LARGE YELLOW RAYS THAT EMANATE FROM THESE BEINGS SYMBOLISE THAT THEY ARE ENGAGED IN THE ACT OF COPULATION OR INTERCOURSE.
- THE ROUND FIGURE AT THE TOP SYMBOLISES A DISCARNATE BEING THAT IS LIVING IN THE KINGDOM OF BLISS. THE YELLOWISH GREY SECTION AROUND THE BEING OF BLISS SYMBOLISES AN ATMOSPHERE THAT IS A MIXTURE OF THE AURA OF THE BEING OF BLISS AND THE COPULATORY AURA OF THE PHYSICAL BEINGS. THIS ATMOSPHERE BRINGS ABOUT THE CONNECTION OR CONTACT OF THE BEING OF BLISS WITH THE CREATION OF THE EMBRYO IN THE WOMB.
- THE CRUCIFORM FIGURE, WHICH IS PARTLY MADE UP OF RAYS AND IS SITUATED BETWEEN THE TWO COPULATORY BEINGS, SYMBOLISES THE CLIMAX OF THE ACT OF COPULATION.
- ORIGINATING IN THE RAYS EMANATING FROM THIS FIGURE THERE IS AN INDIGO-COLOURED THREAD-LIKE FIGURE THAT GOES UP AROUND THE BEING OF BLISS AT THE TOP. IT CONNECTS THIS BEING WITH THE FEMALE BEING AND ANIMATES THE EMBRYONIC MATERIAL IN THE WOMB. AND THUS, BEGINS THE CREATION OF A NEW PHYSICAL ORGANISM.

Fertilization

When the egg has been fertilized with the sperm cell from the man, the process of embryogenesis begins. But it only begins when a discarnate being has added its spirit package to the process. Without this addition, no embryogenesis. The spirit of a discarnate being has to join the fertilized egg in the womb, but in order for the spirit to 'land' with the right parents, there must be a considerable match in wavelength. It is absolutely no chance whom we are born to. The wavelengths must match. This means that the parents and the discarnate being must belong to the same species (cats are born to cats, dogs to dogs, humans to humans, etc.), but there must also be a considerable match in talents, abilities, character traits, dispositions, morals, level of development and intelligence etc. Like attracts like and this is also valid during conception.

The Talent Mass

There has to be a certain amount of identical talent mass for the discarnate spirit and the physical parents to become attracted to each other. For that reason, very warlike spirits will reincarnate with warlike parents and peaceful spirits will reincarnate with peaceful parents. There must be a certain common mass of talents in order for attraction to take place. However, the match will never be 100%. There will always be character traits and talents in a child that none of the parents have. This is mainly due to the fact that each individual has so many talents that a total match is impossible.

There will be talents in a child that none of the parents have because we do not, as is now the general way of seeing things, inherit our talents from our parents. We cannot, through inheritance, receive talents that we ourselves have not developed or indeed worked hard to get. When we have a talent, it is because we have practiced and worked hard to get that talent during our former lives on earth. We do not get anything for free via the genes of our parents. We shall look at this aspect later.

When we 'land' with a specific pair of parents it is because there is a certain match between our wavelength and their wavelength. In this way we can say that we 'choose' our parents through the person we have become. It is the joint characteristics of our I or consciousness, together with the accumulated bank of experiences laid down in our fate element, that decides whom we are born to. This process takes place automatically due to the working of the law of attraction. We are 'simply' attracted to those with the greatest match in wavelength.

The Third Party of Conception

In order for a discarnate being to incarnate into a new physical body it needs a small amount of physical matter to get the process started. This small amount of physical matter is found in the sperm and egg cells. As soon as the sperm cell enters the egg, the discarnate being 'joins the party' and takes over the whole process of embryogenesis. The two physical cells cannot do it on their own. They do not have the know-how. All the knowledge of how to create a physical body lies embedded in the spirit package and fate element of the incoming soul. The incoming soul has been to the physical plane many times before and it has a lot of practice in how to create a physical body. It has its fate element full of talents for bodily creation. These talents are embedded in the fate element as an automatic function, just like the many automatic functions we have such as heartbeat, digestion, breathing, our ability to walk etc. An automatic function is something we can do without the brain and the will being involved. It is something we have done so many times that a talent kernel has taken over the function, so that we do not actively have to think about it.

The incoming soul now puts these talents to work and it will create a new physical body entirely in its own favour, which means just as it fits its own purpose. This means that it will pick and choose in the genetic material put at its disposal by the parents. It will activate the genes it likes and deactivate the ones that it does not like. Like a director it will orchestrate cell division, the creation of organs and the whole of the embryogenesis. It will, as just mentioned, do it in its own favour, and this means it will create a body the way it wants it, depending on its pool of talents and taking its point of departure from where it let off the last time it died. Each time we reincarnate we start our physical life at the level of development we had reached the last time we died. We simply continue our physical journey and none of the things we learned in our previous lives are lost. The incoming soul is fully aware of this and it will create a body that fits the level of evolution it has reached.

Let us just at this point repeat that the belief sustained in the eastern religions that we can reincarnate into sub-human species such as snakes or rats is a complete misconception. It cannot be done, because there is too little vibrational match between two different species. We cannot jump between species between two incarnations. And furthermore we can only move forwards in evolution, not backwards. For each life we live, we become a better, more moral, more intelligent, more humanitarian and more beautiful version of ourselves. For each life we live, we move a few steps closer to the goal of becoming Man in the Image and likeness of God.

With regards to the initiation of the embryogenesis it has been acknowledged by science that during the first days after fertilization information is added to the otherwise ignorant sex cells. Suddenly there is information present in the zygote (the fertilized egg) that was not there before. It has puzzled scientists where this information came from. After cell division, suddenly the cells migrate to form three layers: the ectoderm, the mesoderm and the endoderm layers. How do the cells know to make this differentiation? Where does the impetus and information come from? From the three layers the cells now differentiate into the 200+ different cells types that a human body consists of. How is this at all possible if there is no organizer and an 'architect' behind this highly complex process?

From the two sex cells the embryo/foetus develops into a multi-billion cell structure, organized in the most appropriate, logical and well-functioning way. How would that be at all possible without an organizing principle? Somebody has to tell the cells how to develop, where to migrate to, what type of cell to become and what function to undertake. No wonder that this miracle has remained a mystery to humankind as long as we did not factor in the incoming soul who, in its fate element, has all the needed information for embryogenesis. It has this information because it has accumulated it during thousands and thousands of previous

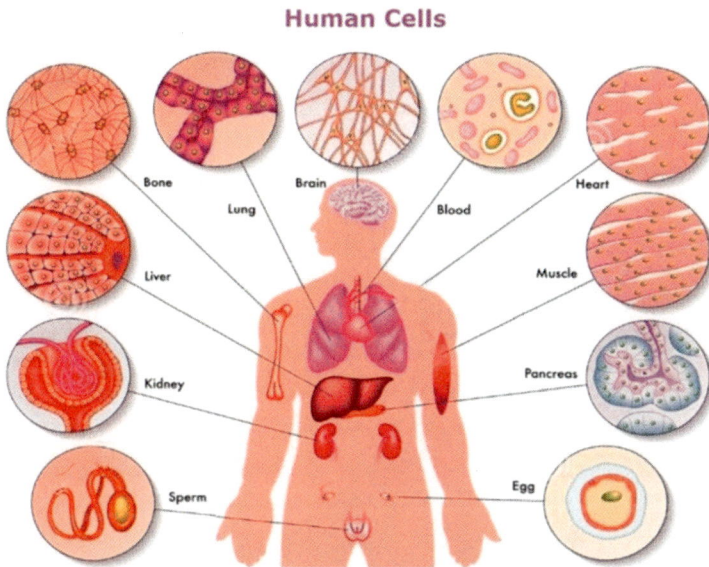

This is just a small selection of the 200+ different cell types in a human body

incarnations where it slowly has learned to master the process. It has the know-how of embryogenesis stored in its fate element as an automatic function. An automatic function is something that we know how to do without being consciously aware of it, just like our heartbeat, breathing, bowel function, walking etc.

If the discarnate being did not 'join the party' and participate in the process of embryogenesis, it is impossible that a new embryo could be created. The egg cell and the sperm cell cannot do the job alone. They may deliver the genetic basic material, but they do not have the know-how for embryogenesis. There is simply not enough information present in the two sex cells to start and complete the creation of the embryo.

It is research from the Department of Zoology, University of Oxford, that has revealed that information is added in the course of the process. This added information is quite a mystery to science, because they do not operate with the spiritual element. They have no idea where the added information comes from. But it comes from the incoming soul, who, as already mentioned, has all the needed know-how embedded in its fate element. If there were no incoming soul, no new baby could be created.

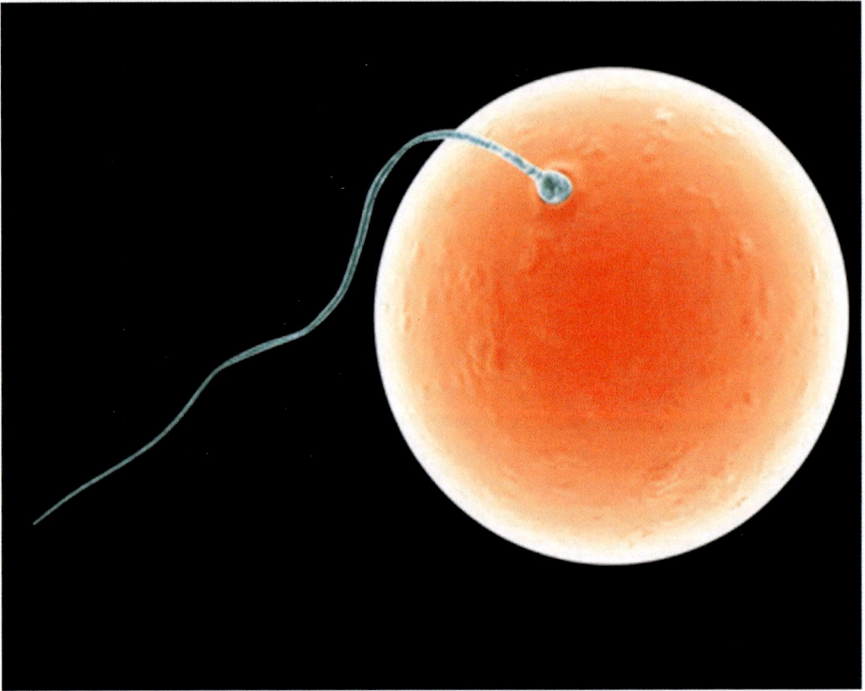

The sperm enters the egg

The incoming soul is already a seasoned being at the point in evolution where we are standing now. It has been to the physical plane in a physical body lots of times before and it is a virtuoso in creating a physical body. It knows how it is done and like a conductor it organizes the cells, first into the ectoderm, the mesoderm and the endoderm layers and later into the various cell types that a human body consists of.

No new being could come into existence without the information embedded in the spirit of the incoming soul.

Already in the womb the foetus has a lot of skills and abilities, and it will make use of those as soon as it can. Why not? It can already hear and sense because these abilities were already well developed in its last incarnations. It knows how to move its limbs, so it will kick and practice

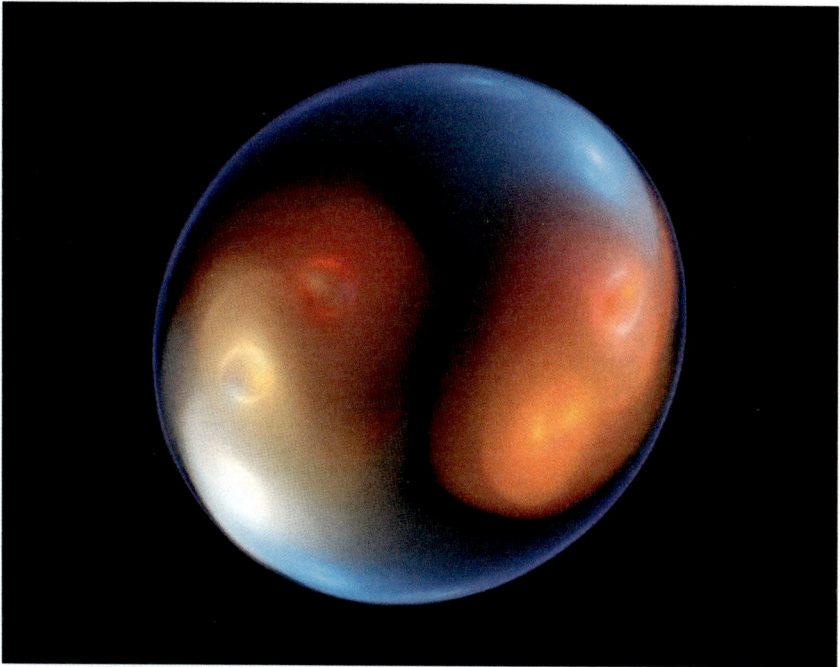

Zygote or fertilized egg. The cell division and creation of a new physical body only starts when the discarnate spirit has joined the process

muscle control already long before birth. The baby whom the mother carries is not the helpless, ignorant being that is the mainstream narrative. It is a being that has already come a long way in evolution and it is not the 'tabula rasa' that we have been told. It is an old soul ready to start on a new adventure on the physical plane.

Today it is acknowledged that the baby can hear already in the womb several months before it is born, it is acknowledged that it can sense its mother's moods and react to them. How would that be possible if the baby had no previous experience of hearing and sensing?

Once the baby has been born it exhibits a lot of skills that would be impossible if it really was the 'tabula rasa' that is believed by most people. If a new-born baby was born with no previous experience, it would not be able to hear, taste, see, feel, smell, make sounds, express individuality and personality, not to mention have a consciousness. Where would the consciousness of the new child come from, if it was not a part of the spirit package that now reincarnates? The baby has personality and

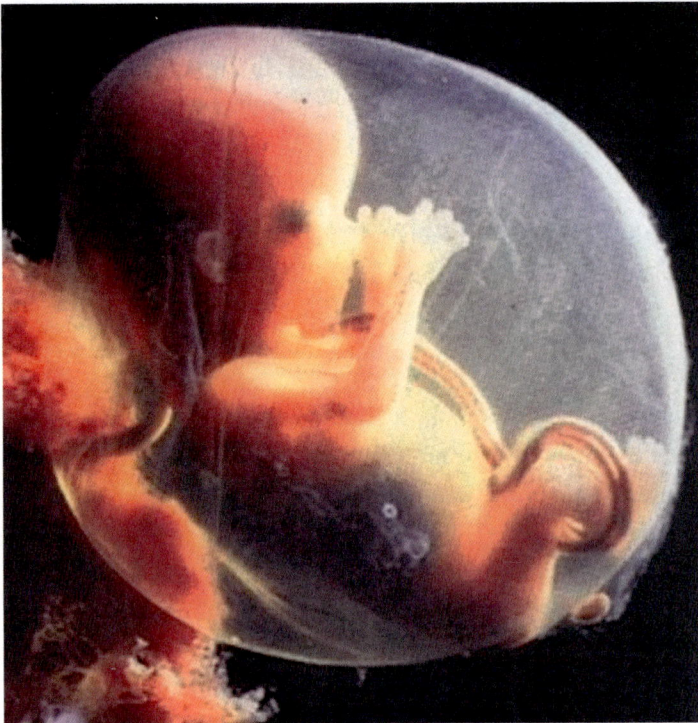

The foetus after 9 weeks

specific preferences already at birth, and how would that be possible, if it really was a tabula rasa? The new-born baby is already a seasoned and experienced being at birth and now, in its new vehicle, it has to get used to operating its new body.

The baby quickly learns how to do a lot of other things too. After a few months in the cradle it quickly learns to crawl and then to walk and talk etc. How could it learn to do these things so quickly, if it did, in fact, not know already? Crawling is a good example. The child rolls on to its stomach, gets up on its arms, bends its legs and crawls. Crawling is an exceedingly complicated activity, which includes a lot of different muscle groups and a lot of coordination. How would this be possible, if the child did not already know how to crawl? Crawling implies an exceedingly complicated coordination of different muscle groups, but still, the child generally learns to crawl rapidly and without anybody teaching it how it is done. All the child has to learn is to control its new body. But it already knows which muscles to activate and when, because this information lies stored in the fate element.

When a new child is born, it carries with it the abilities and talents that it has practiced and perfected during former lives. If it did not, how could babies be able to do all the things they do and be very different in regard to character, temperament, skills, intelligence etc.? When children exhibit different abilities, character traits and talents, it is because they have been through different experiences in their former lives.

The Genes

It is generally believed that all our abilities and talents are based in our genes and that our DNA code is a thing 'carved in stone'. The idea was that our DNA defined who we are. It was believed that we were the 'victims' of the genes we carried from our parents. It was also believed that if we could map the human DNA, then we would be holding the key to understanding life. Hence, millions of dollars were spent on the Human Genome Project whose aim it was to map the human genome.

But there was a flaw in the basic assumption, and this flaw was only discovered after years of research. At the onset, it was believed that by mapping the human genome, scientists would be able to determine the origin of most human diseases. The assumption was that all human characteristics could be traced to specific genes, and that one gene would give one effect. This was termed genetic determinism. It was expected that once all genes had been mapped, we would know everything about how a human being was composed.

However, when the preliminary result was published only 25.000 - 30.000 genes had been found. That was way too few to account for the complexity of humans. Only 30.000 genes were found in the human genome where scientists had expected 100.000. Furthermore, the shocking fact was that we humans only have 300 specific genes distinguishing us from a mouse. How could the difference between a mouse and a human be explained in only 300 genes? Well, it could not, so mapping the human genome did not deliver the expected key to understanding life.

The conclusion was that the genes alone do not hold the secret of life. There was something else at play, something that regulated the genetic expression, because the genes alone could not even begin to explain the complexity of life.

Therefore, the hunt was on for the illusive 'regulatory elements'. What were they? Where? How?

Epigenetics

Then the research field of epigenetics arose. Epigenetics is the study of changes in organisms caused by modification of gene expression rather than alteration of the genetic code itself. In other words, the scientists were looking for the element that could change the expression of the gene without changing the nucleotide sequence. The DNA sequence remained the same, but still the gene would express itself differently. This means that a gene is not a stable element, not 'carved in stone', but something that can be changed by outer influences, meaning that non-genetic factors can cause the organism's genes to be either activated or silenced. These changes are called epigenetic changes and they modify how the gene behaves.

Outside factors (epigenetic factors) can influence the expression of the gene, so that it behaves differently than expected. So far, scientists have been looking at outer factors such as food, medicine, chemicals and environmental influences, but what actually determines the gene expression is not well understood.

However, cell-biologist Bruce Lipton claims to have found the 'missing link' in our consciousness or thoughts. In his ground-breaking book "The Biology of Belief" Lipton reveals that his research has shown that our genes and DNA do not control our biology, as had been the traditional assumption, but that the DNA is controlled by our beliefs. Lipton likens a gene to the keyboard of a piano that can be played in many different ways. He suggests that it is our beliefs, consciousness and thoughts that can modify the expression of the gene. This is a showdown with the traditional way of viewing the body as a bio-chemical machine in which we are victims of our genes. If we were ill and suffering from a hereditary disease, then we had just been unlucky and there was nothing we could do about it. But that is not true, says Lipton. We can do a lot;

actually, we can change the way our genes express themselves by changing our thoughts. *We can change our biology with our thoughts.*

This is supported by Martinus. He very clearly states that our thoughts are the most important factor in our biology and health. What we think, we become.

As stated in a former chapter Martinus says that our thoughts are small currents of electricity on very fine wavelengths. This means that when an individual is thinking, a current of fine electrical waves runs through the organism, making thinking identical to an 'electrification' of the organism. This electrification can be likened to a 'filling up' of force or power. This force is, as already mentioned, identical to our life force. Thoughts, consciousness and life force are the same.

Our thoughts are the most important factor in our health, as Martinus says. Our thoughts overrule our genes. The genes do what the thoughts tell them to do. The genes simply do not hold the secret to life as was once believed. A gene is 'just' a recipe for a protein. A protein is a physical substance and it can be modified by thoughts. A physical substance like a protein cannot explain our non-physical abilities such as our talents and skills. Talents and skills have no physical expression, they cannot be found anywhere in the body. They are spiritual entities found in the fate element.

The Incoming Soul

What is needed for the embryogenesis to get started and indeed completed is the information present in the consciousness of the incoming soul. As already stated, the incoming soul creates its new body on the basis of its accumulated talents. It orchestrates the whole process and decides which genes are activated and which are silenced. It creates a body completely in its own favour or to fit its own needs. It is the master of creation in the womb. The genetic material only plays the role of the bricks while the incoming soul is the bricklayer and the architect.

The incoming soul picks and chooses among the genetic material put at its disposal by the parents, and that is why siblings can be so different. If it was only the genetic material that mattered in the creation of a new body, then all siblings would be the same, because they have the same basic genes. But this is obviously not so, and therefore scientists have come up with an extraordinary explanation: It is chance!!!!

Yes, chance! It is chance that decides the outcome of the embryogenesis! We have more than a trillion cells that after 9 months have developed into the 200 plus different cell types that now, when the embryo is ready to be born, have organized themselves into the very complex structure that a human body is. If it really were chance, then it could be likened to the idea that the city of Paris had come into existence through chance! Without a plan, without an idea, without organization and logical thinking. The whole complex creation is due to chance! It is tantamount to believing that a tornado can blow through a scrapyard and assemble a jumbo jet along the way.

No, not a single well-functioning creation can come into existence on the basis of chance.

The spirit of the incoming soul with all its accumulated knowledge and talents, stored in its fate element, is the alfa and omega for embryogenesis. Without the spirit, no new being can be born on the physical plane.

Cloning

Let us just briefly touch upon the question of cloning or copy humans. Many people are afraid or are wondering if we will be able to clone humans or make a copy of a certain human being. Will we be able to create copy human beings artificially in test tubes using the cloning technique? Uh, this sounds like brave new world and is scary to think about.

There is no need to worry, because we will never be able to do that! No, and no. This whole idea is based in great ignorance about the role of the incoming soul in the process of embryogenesis. It is not possible to clone a human being because this idea is rooted in the misconception that it only takes an egg and a sperm cell to create a human being. The idea that we can clone humans disregards the role played by the incoming spirit. As it is the incoming spirit that delivers all the know-how of the process of embryogenesis, no copy of an already existing human being can be created. There are no copies, because no two beings have lived through identical experiences, have developed identical talents and evolved equally far. Just as there are no two snowflakes that are alike, there are no two humans that are alike. There are no copies. There are only originals!

We can put the necessary physical ingredients together and we can even inject the sperm cell into an egg, but we can never produce two clones. That is not possible, because in order for the cloning to result in a new human being, we need the presence of a spirit. We need a spirit or incoming soul to participate in the experiment.

Let us say that we tried to clone a human. We have a really nice and good human being that we would like to have a replica of. So, we take the necessary cells and join them together and then we wait and see. Let us say that a spirit is up for the game and seeks reincarnation in the fertilized egg and a new baby is born from this experiment. The new baby will, however, never be a replica of the original human, because it is the incoming soul that decides the outcome of the embryogenesis. It is the incoming soul that creates the embryo on the basis of its own talents and plans, so it is only of a minor importance which genes are present. The incoming soul will pick and choose among the genes and it is these epigenetic factors that are decisive for the outcome of embryogenesis. If the researchers were so lucky that a child was born on the basis of the cloning technique, they would soon be able to see that it was not a clone! What a surprise. We thought we could make a copy of Peter, but the result was not Peter, but Paul. How did that happen? The question cannot be answered without the incoming soul. The supposed clone will not be a clone of the original human. It may have the same genes, but as the genes are modified and adapted to the needs and wishes of the incoming spirit, it will not be a clone.

And anyway, we already have quite a lot of ´clones´ in the shape of identical twins running around. They may look alike but it is an irrefutable fact that identical twins are not identical with respect to personality, character traits, talents, habits, preferences etc. They are not clones because two different spirits inhabit the two bodies created on the basis of the same genetic material. And to the great surprise of the researchers, identical twins do not have identical DNA. There are differences and of course there are, because it is the incoming soul that manipulates with the genetic material and activates and turns off certain genes.

Dolly

But the sheep Dolly then! Is that not a clone? No, it is not. Two different spirits inhabit the clone and the original. But because it is difficult to tell the difference in character traits and personality of two sheep, they have been believed to be replicas of each other. The sheep are a long way behind the humans on the ladder of evolution and they have not yet had time to develop into noticeably different individuals. They are still very much flock animals. So, Dolly and her clone were believed to be identical, but they are not, because two different spirits inhabit the two bodies.

It is impossible to create a replica of any living being. We are all totally unique. We are unique because we are all a result of our gathering of experience in former lives, and no two beings have had completely identical experiences. Remember that we are talking about experiences gathered over millions of years. All those experiences have shaped us into the person we are today. There is no replica of you running around anywhere. We are all totally unique.

Our Children

We have a tendency to think of our children as little people who belongs to us. We think we have created them and now they are ours. But they are not. Our children are only ours inasmuch we have had the privilege to be their parents. Our children belong to life itself and they are here in our midst and we care for them and love them, but they are not here to be a prolongation of us. They are here with their own agendas. They are here with their load of talents that they are going to put to work to create their new physical body, and they are here to get on with their development.

We are not being fair to them if we put a lot of demands on them and require them to do this, that and the other for us because we are their parents. We cannot decide what education they should take, which jobs they should pursue and whom they should partner up with or marry. We have to let them go and do their things. As we certainly do not know what life lessons they have come down to learn, we should be careful with trying to decide over them and only give advice when they ask for it. We are here to help them on their way, we are not here to decide how they live their life.

But that does not mean that we should not teach them manners and be a good example. Because that is the thing: you teach by your example and not so much by your words. *"Don't do as I do, do as I say!"* is a common remark from parents, but it does not work as well as the examples we set.

When we look at our children and see how different they are, then we must realize that there is something more at play than a chance cocktail of genes. Even siblings of the same sex, who have come from the same genetic material, are so different and have so diverse talents and abilities that there has to be something else at play. We have just not known what it was until Martinus revealed the process of reincarnation and the spirit package. Different spirits inhabit our children and if we ask a three-year-old: *"Who were you when you were big?"* we will often get the most interesting answers. The young children are happy to talk about it and they greatly appreciate being recognized as a mature being and not be treated as an ignorant child.

Think about it: you have been trusted with the care of a precious soul for a few decades and you must do what you can to help that soul on its way on the physical plane. Do the best you can, but do not try to control or decide over your child. It is not your job. But being a loving parent is.

Why Can´t we Remember our Past Lives?

Many people refuse to believe in reincarnation because they think, that if we had lived before, then we would be able to remember those lives.

There are actually children who remember past lives and we shall return to those shortly.

But generally, we cannot remember our past lives. Why is that?

Martinus explains it like this: We are not supposed to remember our former lives when we reincarnate into a new physical body, because those memories would be burdensome for us to carry around. It would not be in our best interest to carry memories around from lives when we were suffering, when we were slaves or were tortured, when we were starving or freezing, living in miserable conditions or working under subhuman conditions or being sacrificed live. Remember that we have millions of lives behind us, so which memories should we be able to remember? No, it is in our own best interest that we cannot actively remember our past lives.

But not to worry! Our past lives are with us in every new incarnation in the shape of the person we have become. We have all been shaped by our former experiences and it is these, together with our talents – the things we have practiced and become good at that define who we are today. We have our fate element with us all the time and based on the information stored there, we can draw on this information in situations in our present life. It is through our former lives that we have reached our present stage of evolution and our morals, our code of conduct, our level of intelligence, our preferences and habits, what we can find it in our hearts do to others, are all a result of our harvest of wisdom in former lives. What we are today is a result of all the lives we have lived before, and we carry the wisdom harvested during those lives with us into each new incarnation. We take the essence of our former lives with us, but not the day-conscious memories.

Points to Ponder from Maria:

Re: The Process of Reincarnation

I think I can make a safe guess that very few, if any, people have ever considered the act of copulation in the way Martinus describes it. It brings a whole new level of spirituality to sex, one that I have not come across in any book I've ever read. Sex and spirituality do not usually make good bedfellows – excuse the pun! If you think of mainstream religions, sex has been considered a sin by so many of them. But in light of what Martinus has shown us, nothing could be further from the truth.

Of course, we are talking about great, mind-blowing sex (not all of it is, as Else has covered) and the power of love in its physical form when we are consumed with love and passion for another person. I had never considered that this could mean that during such passionate acts we were in contact with the very spirit of God! Wow, that concept is sure to cause a big stir! It's also amazing to think of those discarnate beings waiting in the spiritual realm to 'join the party' as Else says. These concepts redefine the sexual act in ways we've just never considered before.

In the same vein, I recommend you carefully read the section 'Do we choose our parents' and study the Symbol No 34 (and as advised, go to Else's website and download and print the Symbol so that you can refer to it frequently as you read the explanation). I can't really add anything of my own here. But I do know for sure that I have never come across a more comprehensive, compelling explanation of the process of conception, fertilization and embryogenesis.

Re: The Genes

For the layperson (like myself!), the biggest takeaway from this section is once again the power of our thoughts. I have read Bruce Lipton's book and was pleased to learn that Martinus supports Lipton's research and that we can indeed change our biology with our thoughts. If we connect this again to the Law of Attraction, that like attracts like, and that we become what we think about all the time, it gives even more credence to the Law of Attraction. Perhaps this explains how very ill people have healed themselves, to the astonishment of established medical experts who said they were 'incurable', beyond medical salvation and had perhaps just months to live. Both Lipton and Martinus show why this is possible and that our thoughts are powerful beyond measure, even to the point of over-riding the genes!

This does rather turn scientific theory on its head, but then science only knows so much. In time it will know more and eventually, I believe, that Martinus' teachings will all be 'discovered' by scientists as their exploration into scientific knowledge continues... knowledge that a simple, uneducated, illegitimate Danish man has already given us. It does make me want to project myself into a future life to see this become a reality!

Re: Cloning

Somehow the idea of cloning a human being (or even a sheep!) always left me feeling uneasy. Something just didn't 'fit' right with me and I was delighted to read Else's section on cloning because it validated my feelings. It is not possible to clone a human (or a sheep!) and it's clear why, when we see that we are all totally unique; each one of us is a unique spiritual entity. I think it's really important for us to internalize this knowledge and embrace the value and uniqueness of our own magnificence. Never compare yourself to others, because, as I have often said, to do so devalues and demeans who you truly are. When you realize how powerful you are just to *be here* and how much you have evolved through living so many lives, is it not truly awe-inspiring?

If you look back over our history, you will realize that in spite of current wars and global strife, we are a much kinder race that we were. Consider the savagery, brutality and disregard for life that was once common. Think of the Romans feeding men to lions whilst thousands of spectators cheered and clapped, kings and queens beheading people without a shred of remorse, and even relatively recent atrocities such as slavery and the Holocaust. The human race has, by and large, evolved to now know that this kind of brutality and disregard for human life is no longer acceptable. So in spite of the present-day horrors, things are better than we might imagine. We are getting better, more loving and more thoughtful.

Re: Our Children

This section is very dear to my heart. As a Clinical Hypnotherapist and Life Coach, I deal with clients all the time who have suffered because of their parents. Many have been horribly abused, but abuse can come in much subtler forms and still destroy the child's right to live their own life, on their own terms. Way too many parents want their children to live their lives according to the parents´ wishes and dictates, which completely ignores that child's right to forge their own path, make their own mistakes and learn their own lessons. The adult child often harbours deep-seated resentment, depression, trauma and a host of other negative emotions as a result of not being allowed to grow into the person they were meant to be. Parents need to understand that though they gave physical life to their child, they do not own the rights to that child's life for evermore. They need to step back, set good examples, and be there to support their offspring when it's needed. In doing so, millions of people would be free to be themselves and emotional and mental health issues would rapidly cease to exist.

Think about your own parents. How have they influenced you against (or for) your true heart's desires? Do you believe that you have the right to live your life on your own terms, and what can you do to make that a reality for you if it isn't your reality now?

Re: Why can't we remember past lives?

When you consider that you often can't remember what you dreamt about the previous night, or where you went on any given day a week before, is it any wonder that you can't remember your past lives? And as Else says, it would be very confusing if you could! Most of us have more than enough going on in this life to cope with. The fact that we can't remember them is a blessing and a mechanism of protection.

Of course, if you really want to delve into your past lives, this can be done with hypnosis. Usually people seek past life hypnotherapy for three reasons: curiosity, to find healing, or to find insights into this life's purpose. Many people have found incredible healing by means of past life regression. Again I refer you to Dr Brian Weiss if you are interested in examining your past lives. He does have a live session on YouTube you can try out for yourself.

You can also check out some of the books that Else has referenced if you want to delve more deeply into research for yourself. It's fascinating!

6. The Evidence

Is there any evidence that we have lived before? Indeed, there is. When it comes to scientifically presented evidence for reincarnation we are in debt to the late Ian Stevenson, M.D., Professor of Psychiatry at the University of Virginia School of Medicine. All through his professional life Stevenson gathered more than 3000 cases of children who remembered past lives. His work has, among others, been published in the books: ´Twenty Cases Suggestive of Reincarnation´ and ´Where Reincarnation and Biology Intersect´.

Children Who Remember Past Lives

This chapter will present several fascinating cases of children who remember former lives. These children not only remember a variety of details from a former life, but most of them can even remember what they were called, where they lived and who their family was. Some even carry scars which are associated with memories of wounds inflicted in a previous life. As the memories of the children cannot be explained as having been attained through any type of "normal" source, they are a strong case for reincarnation and contribute to undermining the mainstream concept that we only live once.

In his book "Twenty Cases Suggestive of Reincarnation" Ian Stevenson presents some very convincing cases of children who remember past lives. The twenty children, whose stories are presented in the book, all have memories not pertaining to their present lifetime, and they can in most cases give the name and in all cases some characteristics of the person whose life they remember. They can recount intimate details from the previous life and these details have been confirmed to be true through interviews with family members of the previous personality. All the cases in the book are fully documented with a strictly scientific approach, everything has been checked and double-checked, and the results are presented in a completely matter-of-fact way. The twenty cases have been gathered from many different locations such as Ceylon, India, Alaska, Brazil and Lebanon.

To Stevenson a case has been verified when he finds a child with spontaneous and detailed memories from a life which in details fits with that of a deceased person. The memories have to be related to the life of one (and only one) deceased person. For a case to be verified it is a prerequisite that the child has had no possibility to have acquired information about the deceased person in a normal way. In other words, a case is verified only when both sides of the equation fit and when the only logical explanation of the knowledge that the child has is a memory from a former life.

A case typically begins when a young child around the age of 3 without any kind of prompting begins to speak of a former life. The child will mention people and places that nobody in his family has heard about before and will in certain cases describe details of his/her former death. The child will be quite insistent in claiming to have a different name and he will tell his amazed parents that he is, in fact, somebody else. He may also say that he has other parents or a wife and children that live in a different city or even a different country. The child continues to talk about his former personality for several years, generally to the great annoyance of his parents. When Stevenson, through a network of helpers, learns about such a child, he visits the child and takes notes of all the data that the child recounts. If possible, Stevenson arranges that the child be taken to the town where he says he lived before. On this visit, the child will then typically lead the way through the streets to his former home and will spontaneously recognize and greet persons like old friends, calling them by their pet names. When the child enters the house, where he lived before, he will comment upon changes in the decoration of the house, he will ask about persons and things that he thinks are missing and remember events from the past. In certain cases, he reveals knowledge about secret hiding places or where the family gold is hidden, about family debts or old scandals, all of which are confirmed to be true by the surviving family members. The child knows nothing about the time after the death of the former body – his or her memories are limited to the span of the specific former life.

In "Twenty Cases" Stevenson relies mostly on oral reports, based on memory, from his subjects and informants. However, in his book "Where Reincarnation and Biology Intersect", he adds yet another and much more palpable piece of evidence for having lived before: Scars and birthmarks on the body of children who remember a past life.

An example of such a case follows. Ian Stevenson recounts:

"The case of this group for which I will present most detail is that of Chanai Choomalaiwong, who was born in central Thailand in 1967. His parents lived separately, and Chanai was at first raised by his mother and maternal grandmother, who owned a duck farm. From the age of 2, he lived alone with his grandmother at a place called Nong La Korn. When Chanai was born, he was found to have two birthmarks, one at the back of

his head (Figure 4) and one at the front, above his left eye (Figure 5). At that time his family had no understanding of their possible origin.

When Chanai was about 3 years old, his grandmother noticed that when he played with other children he would pretend that he was a teacher and would also say that he had been a teacher in his last life. He said that he was called Bua Kai and had been shot and killed while on the way to his school. He said that he had parents, a wife, and children. He began to beg his grandmother to take him to Bua Kai's parents and claimed that he could show where they lived at a place called Khao Phra.

Eventually, when Chanai was still less than 4 years old, his grandmother decided to take him to Khao Phra. They went by bus to a town called Khao Sai, which is near Khao Phra. There Chanai led the way to a house. They entered, and Chanai recognized an elderly couple as "his" parents. They were the parents of a schoolteacher called Bua Kai Lawnak, who had been murdered in 1962. They examined Chanai's birthmarks, and these, together with his statements, impressed them sufficiently so that they invited him to return. On a second visit to Bua Kai's family Chanai recognized other members of the family and also some objects that had belonged to Bua Kai. He answered questions about Bua Kai's possessions with impressive accuracy...

On the morning of January 23, 1962, Bua Kai left home to go to his school on his bicycle. On the way, he was shot in the head from behind and died almost instantly". (*Stevenson:* "Where Reincarnation and Biology Intersect" pages 38-39).

In his account, Stevenson goes on to relate how a doctor specified the position of the entrance and exit wounds from the bullet on Bua Kai's body. When Stevenson met Chanai, he examined and photographed his birthmarks (hence the references to figures 4 and 5). The positions of the birthmarks of Chanai were identical to the entrance and exit wounds of Bua Kai.

In this case, as in the other cases from "Where Reincarnation and Biology Intersect", there is substantiated and palpable evidence to support the informants' claims about previous lives. Not only can the informants recall episodes from the previous lives, but the body of the reincarnated person bears visible marks inflicted on the body of its former personality.

It should be noted that when a child remembers a former life it is mostly due to the fact that the former life ended violently. It is as if the violent death impresses itself on the consciousness, and the day-conscious memory persists after reincarnation. In most cases it is children who died violently in their last incarnation that remember their past life. A person who has lived a long life and died peacefully is unlikely to actively remember a past life.

Ian Stevenson passed over in 2007, but research into children that remember past lives is still going on and has been further prompted by the American researcher and author Carol Bowman's work, published in "Children's Past Lives. How Past Life Memories Affect Your Child". In this book, Carol Bowman relates a large number of cases, mostly from the USA, collected by herself in which children spontaneously remember past lives.

Small things can trigger past life memories in a child such as in the case where a father was watching TV, when his 3-year-old son passed him on his way upstairs to bed. On TV there was a history program and the boy pointed to the screen and said: *"That's Abe Lincoln, isn't it? I fought for him in the war"*. The boy then proceeded to describe his life as a soldier in the American Civil War with such minute detail and in such a mature voice that his father became convinced that he was remembering a past life.

In her book "Return from Heaven," Bowman concentrates on cases of children who reincarnate into the same family from which they died. Carol Bowman says:

"I can usually spot the genuine cases after a few minutes of talking to the parent, because they fit the pattern I've learnt to trust as signs of a past life memory. In fact, it's amazing how often I see the same types of things in case after case: the very young age when the child first speaks of the past life, the serious and matter-of-fact tone, statements with specific references to the past, as well as the behaviors and physical characteristics that are consistent with the life of the deceased...The large number of similar cases I see is not the only thing that points to a real phenomenon. It's also <u>how</u> the parents are convinced, often against their will. Most of the people who seek me out have no prior belief in reincarnation. The idea that a relative could be born to their family is the furthest thing from their minds. Many are initially upset by what they are witnessing in their child because it rattles their belief that "we only live once" and flies in the face of their religious training" (Bowman: "Return From Heaven", pages 49-50).

In this book Bowman recounts a number of cases of children who reincarnate into the same family from which they recently had died. It could be mothers that reincarnate as their own granddaughters, uncles that reincarnate as their own nephews or even children who died young that are reborn to the same mother. The cases are very convincing, and they bring great joy and comfort to the parents who through typical behavioral patterns or birthmarks recognize a deceased family member in their young child.

Consider the following case. The woman who recounts her story, Candy, had lost her mother, Artise, to cancer. Artise had been a high-spirited woman who loved to sing, dance and perform. Candy later became pregnant and gave birth to a healthy baby girl whom she named Kari.

One day, when Candy was shopping in the supermarket with Kari, a clairvoyant woman passed her. The woman then asked Candy if she realized that it was her mother, who had come back as her daughter. But Candy already knew because Kari looked just like her grandmother from the moment she was born. Everyone in the family saw the similarities between Kari and Candy's mother Artise. Before she could walk Kari would sit in her playpen and hum old tunes that Candy did not recognize, but Candy's grandmother, Dolores, knew them and could tell that they were songs Artise used to sing.

Later the following episode took place:

"One day Dolores and I went shopping and, of course, we took two-year-old Kari with us. We were driving down the road with her in the back in her car seat humming merrily as usual. Suddenly she burst into song, singing the old standard "Chattanooga Choo Choo" word for word! I was so unnerved I couldn't drive. I pulled over so I wouldn't wreck the car. We all just sat there on the side of the road until Kari finished all the verses. My poor grandmother was almost in hysterics, muttering, "Oh, my God! Oh, my God!"

I asked Dolores, "Didn't Grandfather always sing that song?" I remembered him singing it to us when we rode in his car.

"Yes", she said, "it was one of his and Artise's favorite songs". There was no way Kari could have known the verses. She had never heard the song before, not from the radio or TV — it's not a song you hear anymore. And she didn't get it from me. I was vaguely aware of the song, but I sure didn't know all the verses and neither did Dolores. But this little two-year-old knew all of them, every line!"

Bowman: "Return from Heaven" page 94.

Candy is absolutely convinced that her daughter is her mother reborn. The similarities between the two personalities are so striking and the sensation of being with the same person so convincing that Candy has become convinced about reincarnation.

The number of cases gathered by Carol Bowman and the impossibility of "explaining away" the minute, correct details that the children recount are very convincing and a very interesting read, which certainly suggest that we have indeed lived before.

We would also like to present the following example from the Icelandic researcher Erlendur Haraldsson´s book : "I Saw the Light and Came Here"

The child Nazih from Lebanon made several statements about a former life in front of several family members. He said, *"I am not small, I am big. I carry two pistols and 4 hand grenades. I am a fearless strong person, I have a lot of weapons. My children are young and I want to go and see them"*. To his mother he said: *"My wife has more beautiful eyes than you"*. He described how he was shot by armed people. At the age of seven the parents finally yielded to Nazih's persistent requests and took him to the town, where he claimed to have lived before. He directed them to a street, where he said he had lived before. There they met a young widow and her children. The life of her deceased husband Fuad corresponded to that of Nazih´s memories. Nazih correctly answered questions about Fuad that only the wife and Fuad knew. Nazih also recognized some of Fuad's possessions and he reminded Fuad´s wife of events they had experienced together.

There is no way within our traditional understanding of the world to account for Nazih's memories. He could not have accessed the detailed knowledge about Fuad's life through any known channels, as he had never been in contact with anybody who had known Fuad. Also, there is no way to explain the intimate details he shared with Fuad's widow other than reincarnation. But, then, reincarnation is what we all do. It is only, however, in special cases such as this one that actual memories from the former life spill over into the new incarnation. In this case Fuad had been shot, so again it seems that in cases of a violent death the memory of a former life spills over into the next.

As we saw in previous chapters the spirit package with consciousness / I / life force is released from the physical body at death, but it does not cease to exist. It lives on as a spiritual entity with its consciousness and sense of self intact. The consciousness holds all the information that the I has accumulated during a whole number of incarnations, and this means that personality, character traits, talents, habits and dispositions, tastes and dislikes, level of morality, level of intelligence etc. are transferred from one incarnation to the next. We are simply the same being from one incarnation to the next. For each life we live, new experiences are gathered, and new abilities are added in the shape of talents, but the core of the being, the I, is the same from life to life. We learn and become better, wiser, nicer, and more human for each life we live. The aim with our development is, as already mentioned, to graduate as perfect human beings, devoid of all "low" tendencies, such as intolerance, hatred, envy, greed, egoism, negativity etc.; let it here just suffice to say that it is, indeed, an old soul with all its accumulated wisdom that reincarnates into the new baby.

Also, Martinus explains that scars and birthmarks can be transferred from one body to the next and that they will be especially conspicuous when the scars are the result of fatal wounds. If a wound was so serious that it was the cause of death in the previous incarnation, then the body has not had time to heal the wound, and the imperfection of the wound will be transferred to the next body, simply because its mark will have affected the ability for bodily creation. If, on the other hand, a person has a wound that has healed, this wound will not be visible, or not very clearly visible, on the next body because the healing process has been completed so that no scar will appear on the next body.

Child Prodigies

It was stated earlier that we become good at things through practice. When we practice, a small talent kernel is formed in our supraconsciousness and the more we practice, the better we become at performing the activity in question. When we have practiced a lot, we can become really good at performing the activity, indeed we can become geniuses.

The only way to become good at something is to practice. We do not become good at anything by just lying on the sofa. When we are born with talents for certain things, it is because we have worked hard to achieve those talents. The talents we have, have not just fallen out of the sky into our laps.

When we know that we only become good at things through practice, then it is obvious that when we are born with talents, we have to have been in a place where we can have practiced those talents. And such a place can only be a former life. What else can it be?

Our talents are evidence that we have lived before. But, you may now say, I believe I simply inherit my talents form my parents. Yes, that is the mainstream narrative and it can hold when we have talents that we have in common with our parents or grandparents. But what about the talents we have, that we do not share with our parents or grandparents? How can they be explained? Well, the thing is that science has never attempted to explain this and it doesn't even have a theory.

But Martinus says that we inherit our talents from ourselves, so to speak, and that we do not get any talents for free through inheritance. When we are born to parents with a certain similarity in talent mass this is due to the law of attraction. Via our vibration and wavelength, we are attracted to parents with a certain match in talents.

The ability to perform a certain task is laid down in our fate element. This is like a memory chip that holds the information about how a certain task is performed. We know it works like that because every time we start anew on the thing we have been practicing, the level of perfection, we had reached the last time we practiced, will still be with us. We do not have to start from scratch each time. There is a place where the know-how about how to perform the activity is stored. As already mentioned, Martinus calls this place a talent kernel. Our talent kernels accompany us all through life and because they are stored in the fate element, they also accompany us beyond death. We take our talent kernels, with all the stored information about how a certain activity is performed, with us into our next incarnation.

The validity of the above claim is easy to ascertain because nowadays a lot of hugely talented children have been filmed and can now be watched on e.g. YouTube. We have collected some examples with links to where the children performing can be seen.

Genius musicians

Amira Willighagen

Amira was born on March 27, 2004. In 2013, at the age of 9, she won the sixth season of Holland's Got Talent.

Amira impressed the judging panel with her version of "O mio babbino caro" from Puccini's opera Gianni Schicchi. Within seconds the judges were staring in awe and disbelief. One of the judges immediately called her an old soul. Her performance rapidly became a YouTube hit with over 36 million views as of June 2015. She won the competition with over 50% of the viewer vote.

She had never taken any singing lessons, but still she sings like a diva. Interestingly, she chose one of Maria Callas´ signature songs: ´O mio babbino caro´ and her voice is as great as Callas´. It is, of course, not possible to say whether she is Callas reincarnated, but she is certainly a great soprano. Her singing talent is so amazing that it could not have been developed in the 9 years she lived until her debut. It is a clear indication of reincarnation.

The following link is to her performance in Holland´s got talent.

https://www.youtube.com/watch?v=qDqTBlKU4CE

Please go and watch for yourself. It is an awe-inspiring performance that will give you goose bumps.

And here is the link to Maria Callas performing the same aria.
https://www.youtube.com/watch?v=s6bSrGbak1g

Tsung Tsung
This boy from Hong Kong is an absolute piano virtuoso. He started playing the piano when he was three years old and he was only four when he performed the two ´songs´ on the link.
https://www.youtube.com/watch?v=omuYi2Vhgjo
Here he performs Rimsky Korsakov´s very difficult ´The Flight of the Bumblebee´ at five years old.
https://www.youtube.com/watch?v=8snJ4zRhQ9g
Tsung Tung´s talent is so great that he was invited to play at the Ellen DeGeneres show.

Martinus says that reaching the level of perfection of a piano virtuoso will typically take 3- 4 incarnations of diligent practice. It is not a small feat and absolutely nothing anybody can just be born with without having practiced it before. It is also not something that can be found in a gene!

Indian boy
This is an absolutely awe-inspiring performance by a very gifted young Indian pianist.
https://www.youtube.com/watch?v=rsTUVk1y6Zl

Genius painters

Kieron Williamson

Kieron Williamson was born in 2002 in the United Kingdom. He started painting when he was five years old. It soon turned out that he had an extraordinary talent for painting. In 2009 he had his first public exhibition in a small gallery in Holt, Norfolk, the UK. The exhibition was a complete sell-out as were all later exhibitions. His work quickly became collector's items and he was rocketed into the world's spotlight. His work has been compared to that of Monet and he has been nick-named Mini Monet. However, his great idol is Edward Seago and his work has a marked resemblance to that of Seago. At the age of ten he had already made 1,5 million pounds from his paintings.

Read more about Kieron and see some of his amazing work here: http://www.kieronwilliamson.com/

Bales and sails, by Kieron Williamson 2016 when he was 14 years old

Arkiane Kramarik

Arkiane Kramarik was born in 1994 in Illinois, USA. She began to draw when she was 4 years old and she was completely self-taught. Her extraordinary talent for drawing soon became apparent and at the age of ten she appeared at the Oprah Winfrey show. By the age of 12 she had completed 60 large paintings.

`Love´ painted by Arkiane at age 13

The following clip is a short introductory video about Arkiane:
https://www.youtube.com/watch?v=8_hr-a-VfSw

You can see a longer video here about Arkiana´s story:
https://www.youtube.com/watch?v=4VEs6MfkFzo

On her website you can see some of her work:
https://akiane.com/

Arkiane has an extreme gift that she could simply not have developed in this life. She is also very spiritual and has a very close connection to the divine. Certainly, she has a talent so amazing that any other explanation than reincarnation is unlikely.

The smartest kids in the world

Today being a child prodigy is not all that unusual. This is due to the fact that very gifted beings with a full load of talents in their fate element reincarnate here on Earth. The reason that they have so many talents is that they have lived many incarnations and have accumulated and refined a number of skills in their former lives. Their intelligence is so high that some of the kids joined Mensa at the age of 3. Some could read at the age of 2 and taught themselves foreign languages from their iPad. Some could solve math problems before they had been taught at school and one finished his doctorate at the age of 15.

It is obvious that these very gifted children come into this world with a baggage full of knowledge, and there is only one place they could have learned this: in former lives. It is impossible to explain the extremely high levels of gifts, knowledge and insight that these children have without taking reincarnation into consideration.

The existence of these highly talented children is actually a reflection of how far we have come in our evolution. When more and more people on the planet exhibit extraordinary talents, then this fact reflects how far we have evolved. This bodes well for the future of the planet because when these gifted children begin to contribute to our societies, we will all benefit.

We shall look at our evolutionary path in the next chapter. But before we do that please watch the following video and be introduced to the child prodigies:

https://www.youtube.com/watch?v=9GkYELp69us

Famous cases of reincarnation

We can also find cases of reincarnation in the past. We have found three famous people whose talents were so extraordinary and so out of sync with their times that they were clearly very highly evolved beings who had reincarnated into times that lay below their actual state of progress. They did, so to speak, go back to the past. They went back in time in comparison to where they belonged, and they did so to teach, entertain and amuse.

William Shakespeare is often called England's national poet. His huge body of work consists of 39 plays, 154 sonnets and some other works. His plays have been translated into every major living language, and are performed more often than those of any other playwright.

Shakespeare was born in 1564 to cultured and well-to-do parents, but his background does not explain how he could master the English language the way he did. He has the largest vocabulary of the English language ever to have been registered and his knowledge of spiritual aspects abounds in his plays. With respect to wisdom and phycological aspects of the characters of his plays he stood far above the norm of his time. His plays reveal a fountain of wisdom that he could not have attained from mere studies in the 16th century.

He came into this world with a huge baggage of insight from former lives and because of the universal truths he reveals, his work is the most quoted of all in English literature, and it has survived the passage of time to the extent that is seems immortal. The aspects of human folly revealed in his work are so universal that most people will recognize them, and his mastery of the language is such that to this day nobody has surpassed it. Shakespeare is indeed an old soul that came down to the physical plane to entertain, amuse and most of all to teach.

Wolfgang Amadeus Mozart composed a very large number of musical works in his short life. He died at the age of 35. It has been a mystery to his posterity how he was able to compose the bulk of work over so relatively few years.

Mozart was born in 1756 and he composed his first pieces of music when he was 4 or 5. He was a child prodigy and could perform extraordinarily well on the piano from he was 4. His father, who was himself a musician, soon recognized Wolfgang's extraordinary talent and helped him write down his earliest compositions. In total Mozart composed more than 600 works, many acknowledged as pinnacles of symphonic, concertante, chamber, operatic, and choral music. He is among the most enduringly popular of classical composers, and his influence is profound on subsequent Western art music.

Even though Mozart's father was also a musician and composer, Mozart's talent was such that his father soon recognized that his son's talent far exceeded his own, and when he saw the works his son produced, he stopped composing himself.

According to Martinus, we do not inherit our talents from our parents, but we have them because we have worked hard to get them through practice during former lives. It is through the workings of the law of attraction that we are born to parents that have a talent mass that to some extent matches our own. Mozart was born into a musical family but his extraordinary talent for musical compositions is his own doing. It takes several incarnations of practice to reach the level of perfection that Mozart demonstrated. He was an old soul who came down to the physical plane to enrich this level of existence with his wonderful music. And he also came to give us something to think about, because who has not wondered from where he got his talent, if we only live once? Those who firmly believe in the one-life theory are hard pressed for an explanation to Mozart´s extraordinary talent.

Hans Christian Andersen is a Danish poet and storyteller. He was born in 1805 to poor parents. His father was a shoemaker and his mother was an illiterate washerwoman. In spite of his humble background Andersen became one the of the world´s most celebrated authors. He is best known for his fairy tales, which have been translated into more than 125 languages. Even today (2018) 213 years after his birth he is the world´s most translated and one of the most beloved authors. He wrote 3381 works, which include plays, travelogues, novels and poems. His most famous fairy tales include: "The Emperor's New Clothes", "The Little Mermaid", "The Nightingale", "The Snow Queen", "The Ugly Duckling", "The Little Match Girl" and "Thumbelina". His fairy tales are so well loved that most children know them and they have become culturally embedded in the West's collective consciousness.

How can a man, whose father had no literary background and whose mother was illiterate, have genes that would enable him to write the huge bulk of work he produced, if he were not a highly evolved spirit who had reincarnated? Where in the genetic material would we be able to find the abilities that enabled him to spellbind a whole world with his writings?

Other examples of men and women whose abilities stood above the general level of knowledge of their times could be: Leonardo Da Vinci, Johannes Vermeer, Jean of Arch, Cristopher Columbus, Hildegard von Bingen, Santa Teresa de Jesus (of Ávila), Jesus Christ, Buddha, Martinus and many more.

Points to Ponder from Maria

Re: Evidence and Child Prodigies

I think Else's examples in these sections speak for themselves. If you are interested in the evidence, check out the books as there are so many. As for the child prodigies, these examples are wonderful and I urge you to check out all the links for yourself. To my mind, there can be no other explanation for such talents. We cannot simply be born with such incredible gifts if we have not somehow honed our skills in previous lives, and brought them here with us into this life.

7. The Master Plan

We have presented the case for reincarnation in the previous chapters. Reincarnation is much more than a belief and it seems logical to conclude that it is a fact, because it explains so many riddles such as: what is the constant of the physical body, where do our talents come from, where do our phobias and fears come from, where do our character traits or the origin of our dispositions come from and what we can find it in our hearts to do to others etc. It also explains how a new body can arise from two sex cells, why death is an illusion and why there is no reason whatsoever to be afraid to pass over. But as reincarnation is likely to be factual, then what is it all about? Why are we here? Is there a reason for our existence? Is there a plan?

Indeed, there is! This plan has been revealed by Martinus and it is the first time in human history that such a master plan has been disclosed. It is a magnificent plan which is much grander than anybody had imagined. It is magnificent because we are eternal beings living in an eternal universe. Eternity is a very long time, indeed a time so long that time itself loses its meaning. Eternity has no beginning and no ending. If it did, it would not be eternal. It always is and always will be. Our existence as eternal beings also has no beginning and no ending. We never stop living.

An eternal existence has to be filled with something. In order for an eternal existence to have meaning we have to have things to do and things to experience. If we did not experience things, we would get bored. In order to fill our eternal existence with things to experience, our lives have been organized in the most brilliant way: we move in circles and spirals through eternity.

One cyclic passage, which will be presented shortly, takes millions of lives to complete. Once we have completed a cycle, we move up one rung of the spiral to a new cycle on a higher level. Around and around and up and up it goes. Before we look at a cyclic passage we must first examine the principle that is fundamental for all perception: the principle of contrast.

The Principle of Contrast

The experience of contrast is of paramount importance to our eternal ability to perceive. If we always experienced the same thing, not only would we get bored, but we would eventually lose our ability to perceive. If we lived for ever in a white room with white furniture and white paintings, we would experience a total 'whiteout', our senses would be dulled and eventually they would stop functioning. In that way life would gradually cease to have meaning. We cannot eternally experience the same and still maintain our ability to perceive.

In order for the universe to exist eternally, it has to have been created in a way that will sustain an eternal existence. If there were only light, then the universe would have to end once all the beings alive in it had experienced the light to the full. When they were completely satiated with the light and had never seen anything else, then their life experience would cease. Then there would be no more to experience and that would be it.

For that reason, there also has to be darkness. We need the contrast to the light in order to keep our senses alive, in order to refresh our ability to perceive, to be able to experience new things and renew our consciousness. Without contrast there can be no eternal existence. Not for us and not for the universe. The universe has been so ingeniously created that it contains contrasts, so that the beings alive in it will eternally have new things to experience. In order for there to be an eternal ability to perceive we need the contrasts of black and white, good and bad, pretty and ugly, rich and poor, love and hatred etc. We need the whole spectrum of possible outcomes, colours and feelings to experience life eternally.

As we move through eternity, we move in cycles. We shall now look at one such cyclic passage, the one we are all living in right now. The passing of such a cycle takes millions and millions of years. In one cyclic passage we experience both light and darkness, just as we do in the circadian cycle and the annual cycle. These 'small' cycles illustrate for us EVERY DAY how the principle of contrast unfolds. After the darkness of night, we are happy that light returns and after the culmination of light and warmth of noon we are happy with the coolness and darkening of night. We know in our own bodies how pleasant contrasts are. As we are witnessing the unfolding of the principle of contrast every day, it can come as no surprise that this principle is also in operation on a higher level. Also there, the principle of contrast is alpha and omega for our experience of life.

So, in the huge passage, that we shall look at now, there is also contrast. During our passage of the cycle there is a period where the beings live in the light and a period where they live in the darkness. In this way they experience contrast during the passing of one cycle. As all cyclic passages have the same principle of contrast via the experience of light and darkness, the eternal existence of the universe has been secured. The eternal existence of the universe has been secured, because there is always something new to experience for the living beings that the universe consists of. In that way our ability to perceive will be constantly renewed and there can never be a total 'whiteout' or at total 'blackout'. Once we have become satiated with the light, we can experience darkness, and when we are satiated with the darkness, we can experience the light.

In the huge cycle, which has been symbolically represented in symbol no. 22, it is so that the light is experienced in the spiritual world and the darkness is experienced in the physical world. The spiritual world is characterized by light, happiness and love. In the spiritual world we live in true bliss and happiness. But because this world of light exists, there also has to be a place, where we can experience contrast to all this happiness and universal love. The place, where darkness can be experienced, is the physical world.

This means that the raison d'être of the physical world is to constitute a place where contrast to the spiritual world can be experienced. As the characteristics of the spiritual world are light, bliss and love, the place of contrast has to be a world characterized by darkness, suffering and unlove. When we are satiated with the light, we need to experience darkness and it is then that we enter the physical plane in physical bodies. It is in the physical world, on a physical planet that we experience the contrast to the light: darkness. As we shall see on the symbol we are right now passing through this darkness, which is characterized by wars, terror, egoism, greed, envy, hatred, killings and unlove. At a certain point this darkness will reach its culmination and then life is not all that fun to live. We are passing this darkness right now, but the culmination of this darkness was probably in the last century with two world wars and innumerable minor wars. And we are not out of the jungle yet, but we are on our way. This darkness will fade, and light is dawning. A bright future awaits us all.

Suffering

When we are passing the darkness, we experience a lot of suffering. It is a great mystery to us humans, why suffering exists. But it does so that we can experience the contrast to the light. Without an experience of darkness, no experience of light. We can only experience as much light as we have experienced darkness. The whole question of our fates will be the subject of our next book in the Nutshell series: Fate and Karma in a Nutshell.

If every single being did not experience suffering, then this same being could not experience light and happiness. Martinus is the only person, who has explained the mission of darkness and suffering. And the darkness is not a punishment from an angry and revengeful God, but ´only´ a necessary prerequisite for the renewal of our eternal ability to perceive.

And just as our thoughts come before each and every human invention and creation (as mentioned in chapter 2), also the physical world has been created on the basis of thoughts from the highest being, or God, as a place where darkness can be experienced by the living beings. The physical world is God´s materialized thoughts in exactly the same way as e.g., a chair is the materialized thoughts of a human being. Everything in the physical world, in micro as well as in macro cosmos, is materialized thoughts. And as mentioned, the mission of the physical world is to constitute a place where the eternal beings can experience darkness and suffering.

In this connection it is important to underline that no being experiences more suffering than any other. We all have to go through the same amount of suffering. Nobody is let off easier than any other. We all have to go through the same to become the same: a real human being or Man in the Image and Likeness of God. But this ´sameness´ in the amount of suffering cannot be seen when we look at life in a one-life perspective. Then it all looks unjust, illogical and unloving. But it is not, because the darkness is in reality camouflaged love, because without the darkness, there can be no light and without the contrast of light and darkness there can be no eternal universe. The basic tone of the universe is love.

If we look at the world as it is today, we see many different fates, and we think that life is very unjust, because one person lives in happiness and another in misery. But that is just a snapshot view. Seen in the larger perspective all fates are levelled out and nobody can understand his fate seen in a one-life perspective. If we live in happiness in this life, it probably means that we have suffered a lot in previous incarnations. Nothing happens by chance and the universe is ruled by the strictest justice.

Let us now look at our present cyclic passage.

A Cyclic Passage Illustrated

In one of his symbols, i.e. symbol no. 22, Martinus has illustrated a cyclic passage. The symbol is called 'The Eternal, Cosmic, Organic Connection between God and the Sons of God'.

The symbol illustrates two main aspects:

1. As the title suggest there is an eternal connection between God and us, the [4]*sons of God.

2. The symbol illustrates a cosmic cyclic passage.

When we look at the symbol we see that the circle, which illustrates a cyclic passage, is divided into 6 coloured sections. The six colours symbolize different basic energies with their corresponding realms. In each of the realms a specific basic energy predominates. In order to complete a cycle, we must pass through each realm:

The red part (energy of instinct) symbolizes the plant kingdom

The orange part (energy of gravity) symbolizes the animal kingdom

The yellow part (energy of feeling) symbolizes the real human kingdom

The green part (energy of intelligence) symbolizes the kingdom of wisdom

The blue part (energy of intuition) symbolizes the divine world

The indigo part (energy of memory or bliss) symbolizes the kingdom of bliss or memory

We suggest that you print out a large copy of this symbol from martinus.dk... go in under engelsk, and then symbols and then no. 22

---

[4] sons of God. Martinus uses the Danish term: 'gudesønner', which literally translated is: 'sons of God'. Obviously, this concept comprises both sexes

Symbol no 22. The eternal cosmic, organic connection between God and son of God

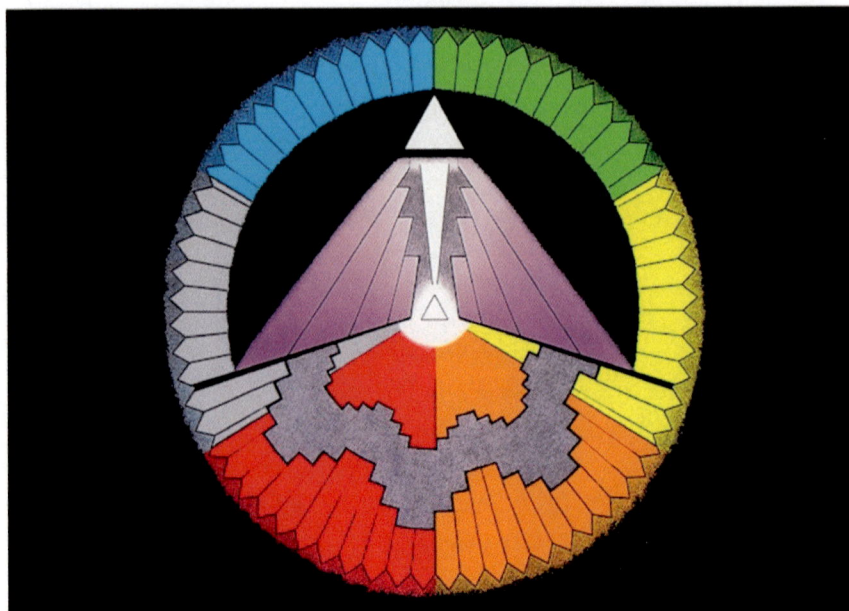

© Martinus Idealfond 1964   Reg. 22

A Summary of Explanation of Symbol No. 22 - The Eternal, Cosmic, Organic Connection between God and the Sons of God – 2 (obligatory official explanation of the Martinus Institute)

THIS SYMBOL SYMBOLISES THE INDIVIDUAL LIVING BEING'S COSMIC CONNECTION WITH THE GODHEAD. MARTINUS DESCRIBES HOW ON THE SPIRITUAL PLANE THERE IS A KINGDOM OF COMPLETELY EVOLVED HUMAN BEINGS THAT CONSTITUTE THE GODHEAD'S PRIMARY ORGANS OF CONSCIOUSNESS. THESE SUPERTERRESTRIAL BEINGS CONSTITUTE A COSMIC GOVERNANCE THAT PROMOTES WORLD REDEMPTION. IT IS THROUGH THE BEINGS THAT MAKE UP THIS GOVERNANCE THAT GOD PERCEIVES THE LIVING BEINGS' PRAYERS AND ANSWERS THEM.

    THE MAIN DETAILS OF THE SYMBOL:

- THE WHITE AND VIOLET PYRAMID SHAPE SYMBOLISES THE ORGANIC STRUCTURE OF THE COSMIC CONNECTION BETWEEN EVERY INDIVIDUAL BEING AND THE GODHEAD.
- THE LARGE TRIANGLE AT THE TOP SYMBOLISES THE I OF THE GODHEAD.

- THE TRIANGLE IN THE MIDDLE SYMBOLISES THE I OF THE SON OF GOD. THE COLOURED SECTIONS CONNECTED TO IT SYMBOLISE THE PHYSICAL BODY OF THE SON OF GOD, WITH WHICH HE EXPERIENCES THE PHYSICAL WORLD.
THE TWO DARK, THICK, ALMOST TRANSVERSE LINES DIVIDE THE SYMBOL IN TWO PARTS:
- THE UPPER PART CONSTITUTES THE SPIRITUAL WORLD.
- THE LOWER PART SYMBOLISES THE INDIVIDUAL UNFINISHED HUMAN BEING SURROUNDED BY THE PHYSICAL WORLD, WHICH CONSISTS OF THE MINERAL KINGDOM (INDIGO), THE PLANT KINGDOM (RED), THE ANIMAL KINGDOM (ORANGE) AND THE PHYSICAL PART OF THE FUTURE REAL HUMAN KINGDOM (YELLOW).
- IN THE LOWER PART THE UNFINISHED HUMAN BEINGS ARE SYMBOLISED IN THE ANIMAL KINGDOM IN THE SECTIONS FROM THE SHORT ORANGE RAYS TO THE YELLOW RAYS.
  - THE TWO SHORTEST RAYS SYMBOLISE THE VERY PRIMITIVE, EARLY HUMAN STAGES, STAGES THAT ARE MORE APE STAGES THAN HUMAN STAGES AND THAT NO LONGER EXIST ON EARTH.
  - THE NEXT RAY SYMBOLISES OUR PRESENT PRIMITIVE HUMAN STAGES, WHICH WILL SOON BE A THING OF THE PAST ON THE EARTH.
  - THE LAST RAY BUT ONE BEFORE THE YELLOW RAYS SYMBOLISES CIVILISED HUMAN BEINGS. THEY ARE GENIUSES AS REGARDS CREATING IN PHYSICAL MATTER.
  - THE HALF-ORANGE AND HALF-YELLOW RAY SYMBOLISES BEINGS THAT HAVE A HIGHLY DEVELOPED FACULTY OF HUMANENESS. THEY ARE ABSOLUTELY NATURAL VEGETARIANS, AND THEY PREFER TO AVOID ALL DISCORD, AND ARE VERY WILLING TO FORGIVE THEIR ENEMIES. THEY BEGIN TO HAVE AN INKLING THAT THERE MUST BE A DIVINE PLAN, AND THAT LIFE MUST HAVE A LOVING MEANING. THEY ALSO RETURN TO PRAYING TO GOD AND DISCOVER THE POWER OF PRAYER.

Let us first look at the aspect of the symbol that explains the eternal connection between God and us, the sons of God.

If you look at the symbol you will see a white triangle in the centre of the circle. This triangle represents us, the living beings. A bit higher up there is a somewhat bigger white triangle. This represents God.

The violet pyramid emanating from God represents the eternal connection between God and the sons of God, us. This connection is in the colour of the mother energy (violet) and it can never be broken. It is always there, whether we are down and out and miserable or happy and grateful. The connection is there whether we feel dejected by God or we feel lifted up. The connection is never severed. We are never forgotten or rejected by God, no matter how badly we have behaved or how much we have 'sinned'. God is always there for us, but probably in a different way than most of us envisage.

Many people think that God is dead and that we don't need 'him' anyway, because we have science. Science will find a way and explain everything to us. But that is asking too much of our earthly sciences. They can only study the physical plane and physical matter, so they are simply not equipped to deliver an explanation to the mystery of life. But they are important in as much as they find answers to a lot of problems and lay the basis for inventions that can help us move forward.

As we evolve, our intelligence grows at the expense of our instinct. Our ability to believe in the religions is closely connected to our instinct. As the instinct loses ground, we are no longer able to believe in the dogmas of the religions. The religions just ask us to believe without presenting a logical reason for this belief. As the religions are not designed to do that, many people take their leave from them and this is happening all over the globe, where all the empty seats in the churches bear witness to the fact that people are no longer able to just believe. They need logical explanations because that is what their growing intellect demands. Because most people think that God is closely connected to the religions they become atheists and godless. They think they can only have God together with the religions. But that is not so. God is above and beyond all religions. 'He' knows that the atheist stage is just a natural step in our evolution, so when we declare that God is dead, it does absolutely not upset 'him'. He knows that this is just a stage and that the eternal connection between God and the sons of God cannot be severed.

The symbol illustrates this connection.

On the symbol we can see that two black lines cut the circle in two. The part that is below the black lines symbolises the physical world, which is where we experience darkness in the shape of suffering, misery, unhappy fates, pain, sorrow, war, misfortune, bloodshed, unrest, slavery, terrorism, starvation and famine, deprivation, poverty and everything that is in contrast to peace and universal love. The part above the two black lines represents the spiritual world. The spiritual world is where we experience light, bliss, happiness, harmony, universal love and everything that is in contrast to the darkness. In the spiritual world we are alive in our spiritual body and in the physical world we have a physical body in addition to our spiritual body. We always have our spiritual body. We ARE our spiritual body as explained in chapter 2.

We can see that the part of the cycle that lies above the two black lines is larger than the part below. This means that during a passage of the cycle, which takes millions of years, we live about 40% of the time in the physical world (with breaks in between, where we return to the spiritual world for a short rest between incarnations as explained in chapter 4) and 60 % in the spiritual world.

The passage of the cycle is what each and every one of us undertakes. It is an illustration of our personal journey. As we travel through the cycle we move anticlockwise.

In the physical world, the part below the black lines, we live in the indigo part (mineral kingdom) for a relatively short time, then for a long time in the red part (the plant kingdom) and an equally long time in the animal kingdom (orange part). Finally, we live for another relatively short time in the yellow part (the real human kingdom).

But no matter where in the circle we are, our connection to God is constant and unbroken. The grey band varies in shape according to the length of the pointed figures, and the length of the pointed figures illustrates different stages of our evolution and also different fates. But, as mentioned already, no matter if our fate is bright and happy or dark and miserable, we are never forgotten or rejected by God. We may think that we are, when we are lying naked, starving and freezing in the mud, but we are not. God is with us also when we experience miserable and dark fates because these unpleasant fates are necessary for our evolution and experience of contrast.

As mentioned, we need to have contrasting experiences in order to be able to perceive eternally. We cannot eternally only perceive light. We need the contrast to light. It is as important to experience darkness in the shape of unhappy and miserable fates, as it is to experience light. One cannot exist without the other. And we have to live through both in order to live eternally. If we only lived in the light, we would not be able to live eternally, because there would be nothing to experience once we had had our fill of the light. As mentioned, an eternal life in the light would be meaningless, because when we had experienced the light fully, there would be no more for us to experience. We would then just live in blindness with nothing to experience.

Martinus explains that the basic tone of the universe is love. We are alive in a totally loving universe where there is no evil. But there has to be both darkness and light. Both the darkness and the light are equally necessary. We cannot have one without the other. Both darkness and light are good things. Thus, Martinus says that we have ´the pleasant good´ (light) and ´the unpleasant good´ (darkness). The darkness with wars, hunger, concentration camps, slavery etc. is very unpleasant to live through, but it is still a good thing, because without it, we would not be able to maintain an eternal existence.

But even during our passage of the worst part of darkness where there are wars, concentration camps, bombings, torture, famine and total misery, God is with us. He is with us because he knows that experiencing these miserable conditions is indispensable for our evolution, for our progress through the cycle. And because death is an illusion, we cannot lose our lives or face eternal extinction. When we pass over, we will enter the spiritual world and live there for a while in our spirit body until we are well rested and are ready to go back to the physical plane to get on with our development.

The Passage of the Physical Part of the Circle

As mentioned, we can see that the circle has been cut in two by the two black lines. The black lines symbolize the limit between the physical realms of the cycle and the spiritual realms. This means that a passage through the cycle implies about 40% sojourn in the physical realms and about 60 % in the spiritual realms. We live more time in the light of the spiritual world than we do in the physical world.

This passage is what every single one of us goes through. It is an illustration of our personal journey through a small part of eternity. The journey never ends, but the passage illustrated here reveals that we experience an endless variety of fates during this journey. There is, so to speak, never a dull moment. But in our passage of the animal kingdom (orange part) there will be pain and suffering. But the pain and suffering are limited to one sixth part of the journey. The rest is pure bliss, as we shall see later.

Let us just repeat that we are primarily spiritual beings. We always have our spiritual body. As we saw in the chapter ´The process of reincarnation´, it is the spirit that creates the physical body. When we are on the physical plane in a physical body, we also have a spiritual body, because this is who we really are. The physical body is just an instrument for the spirit. When we are on the spiritual plane in our spiritual body, we have discarded our physical body, but we are still the same person.

Let us start our passage through the cycle at the black line on the left. This black line symbolizes the point in time when we leave the spiritual plane after a sojourn there of eons of time, after which we yearn for a contrast to the spiritual world. We are more or less desperate to experience something other than this perfect world of spiritual bliss, light and love, so we are eager to go onto the physical plane to experience something else. Hence, we are thrown out of paradise, as this point has been symbolically expressed in The Old Testament.

Indigo Part – the Mineral Kingdom (the energy of memory or bliss)

We start our sojourn on the physical plane in mineral matter, which is illustrated by the indigo colour. The indigo part illustrates the kingdom of bliss and all reincarnation into physical matter takes place from this kingdom. We can see that the major part of this kingdom is on the spiritual plane. At the black line our spirit enters mineral matter, but it does so cautiously, and we still have our consciousness on the spiritual plane. It is as if we put a toe into the physical world and keep our head in the clouds. Our sojourn in mineral matter is only the beginning of our journey in physical matter. We still have our consciousness in the spiritual world, and we cannot feel or sense anything while we gradually enter the physical world via mineral matter. But still this is our preparation for our real entrance onto the physical plane.

We can see that each coloured section is divided into pointed figures. One pointed figure represents a section of our journey. Below the black line we can see two and one third pointed figures of indigo colour. This represents the time we spend in mineral matter – it could well be several hundreds of thousands of years.

Red Part – the Plant Kingdom (the energy of instinct)

Via the intermediate states of lichen and mosses we enter the plant kingdom – the red section. Lichen and mosses practically grow on rocks and they are the stage between mineral and plant matter. We can say that lichen and mosses illustrate the first signs that we are about to wake up in the physical world. We still have the main part of our consciousness on the spiritual plane but gradually it is shifted to the physical plane. This happens little by little as we move through the plant kingdom.

From lichen and mosses we gradually develop into real plants and live as plants all through the red section. In the red section our perception of the physical world is slowly awakened and becomes more and more acute. The plants can vaguely sense the physical world and they can react to it. They can sense heat and cold, light and darkness, rain and drought, and they can close their flowers to the cold and darkness and open them to the light and warmth. They have some kind of movement in their limbs and in that way, we can see that they are alive.

The most beautiful creations that we can see on the physical plane are the flowers of the plants. Because the plant still has the main part of its day-consciousness on the spiritual plane, it is able to reflect aspects of the beauty and perfection of the spiritual plane in its flowers. The colours, shapes and perfumes of flowers are so extraordinary that just looking at them can transport us to a better world. Martinus says: *as long as there is a flower, the idea of a higher world can never be eradicated.* The flowers are a greeting to us from a higher plane of existence and simply walking around in a place where flowers abound can lift our spirit and make us happy.

As it evolves, the plant can sense more and more of what goes on around it – it can sense heat and cold, rain and draught, light and darkness, but it has no day-conscious perception of the physical world: it cannot see and hear, smell and taste... it can only sense vaguely. It can also not feel pain. It still has the main part of its consciousness on the spiritual plane, but gradually, its day- consciousness shifts to the physical plane of existence into its physical body. It is the outer forces from nature such as light, darkness, rain, wind, draught, storms, being eaten by animals and humans that awaken the plant to the physical plane. This means that gradually the plant develops senses with which it can begin to experience the physical world. It still does not have eyes and ears, it does not have nerves and developed feelings, it still cannot move across the ground, but these abilities are evolving in the plant. We see that the plant can open its flowers when the sun shines and close them when it is dark and cold. Thus, it can begin to move its limbs. We also see that the plant has a kind of blood circulation, as it can absorb water from the ground and circulate it to parts of its body. The plant has receptors for light in its leaves, which will evolve into eyes, and in the carnivorous plant we see the beginning of a digestive tract that is under development. We see intermediate stages between plant and animal in e.g. sea anemones, which look like plants but have evolved to the point where they can move slowly across the ground. They are not completely stationary. They can slide along the ocean floor or even swim using their tentacles. The sea anemone is considered to be an animal, but it looks like a flower and it is a perfect example of a species between a plant and an animal.

Orange Part – the Animal Kingdom and the Kingdom of the Unfinished Human Being (energy of gravity)

Once we enter the orange section, we have developed full-blown physical senses with which we can experience the physical world with our day-conscious perception. We no longer have any part of our consciousness on the spiritual plane, now all of our consciousness has been pulled down into the physical body. Our perception is now limited to the physical world. Once that happens, we are no longer plants but animals. All of our consciousness has now shifted to the physical plane and has completely left the spiritual plane. We are now exclusively conscious of the physical plane and are unaware that the spiritual plane exists.

The orange part represents the animal kingdom and we, the humans of today, belong in this section. In the six first pointed sections we are pure animals and in the next 4 2/3 pointed sections we develop from animals to human beings. We begin to walk on our hind legs, we become dexterous with our hands, our intelligence begins to stir and slowly, slowly we evolve towards the human stage.

In the orange section the former plant has now developed its physical senses: it can see, smell, hear, taste and feel. Its nervous system has developed to the extent that it can now feel pain. Slowly the animal develops its ability to feel joy and sorrow, happiness and sadness. Its senses are sharpened, and it can suffer when food is short, and it can feel pain when it is killed. The mentality of the animal is dominated by its instinct of self-preservation. This instinct will enable the animal to survive through many lives and at the basis of this instinct lies selfishness or egoism. In order to survive the animal must manifest selfishness. If it does not, it will perish. The law of the jungle rules.

The first six pointed figures of the orange section symbolize the actual animals. After those the two short pointed figures symbolize the first, very primitive human stages that are more apelike than human. The next figure represents our present nature or 'primitive' people - people who live in the jungle or deserts with no contact to the so-called civilization. The number of nature people is decreasing as they are gradually being absorbed into the societies of the people in the next pointed figure: the cultural human being.

Most people alive today belong to the group of cultural human beings. It is at this precise place that we find ourselves today. We have now travelled through the major part of the orange section and we have reached the point where we have become quite evolved and have created cultural societies. This section is represented by the last whole orange section of the cycle before the section that is both orange and yellow. In the cultural human section, we live in more or less civilized societies with a degree of science and materialistic knowledge. We have laws and a degree of order and justice. We have a high level of technology, which has helped us in many ways: in transport, communication, production and the like. We have schools and hospitals and take care of each other to a certain degree. We are much less selfish than we were when we were pure animals and our survival depended on egoism. Now we are more humane and willing to help each other. Egoism is decreasing at the expense of altruism and empathy.

So, in many ways our mentality has developed away from that of the animal. For each life we live, we become more and more human and humane. Through our sufferings we have developed our ability to feel compassion and love for our neighbour and gradually we move away from the mentality of the wild beast of the jungle, which is characterized by egoism and self-preservation. The more humane we become, the more we are in the process of leaving the animal kingdom. We are on the last stretch of the animal kingdom and we will soon take our departure from it, but we are not quite there yet. We are not there until we enter the yellow section.

The section of the cultural human being is a very mixed ´box´. There are people in it that still have a very ´primitive´ mentality characterized by egoism, greed, lust for power, jealousy, desires to be admired and show off, who can still find it in their hearts to kill other living beings and who think we must eat animals and have wars. But there are also people who are very compassionate and want to help people in need, who advocate peace and harmonious co-existence, who could not participate in killings and therefor do not eat the flesh of other living beings and who emanate universal love. In this way the section of the cultural human beings represents people on many different stages of evolution. But we are all, without exception, approaching the yellow section.

Yellow Part – the Real Human Kingdom (energy of feeling)

Those who are the most all-loving are very close to the last section that is 2/3 orange and 1/3 yellow. This section represents the last part of the animal kingdom. It is where the earthly human being sheds the last traces of its animal tendencies and gradually becomes a real human being. A real human being emanates universal love and s/he loves all other beings. Such a being has finished its passage through the darkness and through its many experiences of life on the physical plane, through sufferings and misery, s/he has developed her/his ability to feel the sufferings of others. Such a being has developed empathy and compassion. It cannot hurt others because in its fate element it has retained an echo of what it is like to suffer. Because of its own passage of darkness, it has enhanced its talent for empathy. And in this way, it is gradually becoming an all-loving being.

When the human being has evolved into an all-loving being, it leaves the orange section and enters the yellow section, which represents the realm of the real human being. The yellow section is defined by the energy of feeling. There are two and 1/3 yellow sections below the black line on the right. These yellow sections represent the real human kingdom on earth.

In the real human kingdom all beings have reached the point where they all emanate universal love and only want to be of service to others. Everybody loves everybody, and all types of cruelty have been abandoned long ago. The riches of the world have been distributed evenly among all humans, so there is no poverty, and everybody is rich. Money has been abandoned and all the riches of the world belong to everybody. There is only one state on the planet: The Earth kingdom. This means that all war has been eradicated and peace on Earth has become a reality. One planetary language will be spoken by all and the local languages will only be spoken locally and if people want to do so. There is no private property, and everybody can enjoy the many cultural arrangements within the fields of art, music, opera, literature, science, travels etc. All hard labour has been taken over by machines and people only work for a few hours a week and only within the fields where they have their interests and talents. Nobody is being exploited. Everybody lives solely on a plant-based diet and because of that all illnesses have been conquered. There is no need for hospitals and carers.

Spiritual science will be the philosophical foundation of this kingdom and many of its inhabitants will have reached the point where they have achieved cosmic consciousness.

We shall reach this kingdom inhabited by real human beings in the course of the next 3000 years, says Martinus. But in only 500 years the last war will be fought on this planet and from then on things will go fast. More and more people will, via their sufferings, have developed into all-loving and compassionate beings and their number will grow because we are all subject to the process of perfection. As we live life after life, we move forwards in evolution and the aim of this process is to become man in the image and likeness of God, as already explained. Once we have reached that point, which is inevitable, because it is part of the master plan, then a kingdom of finished humans will become a reality. An example of a finished human being is Jesus and just imagine what such a kingdom will be like, where everybody behaves like him. It will be such a blessed place that we can hardly imagine the bliss we will all live in there.

Once we have lived in the kingdom of the finished human being for a period of time, we have arrived at the black line on the right. This means that we are ready to leave the physical plane. We have learned all there is to learn there, we have become real all-loving human beings and we have experienced contrast in the shape of the sufferings we lived through during our passage of the animal kingdom, the orange section. We have seen and felt how darkness can manifest itself, and with this fresh in our consciousness we are ready to re-enter the spiritual world. This is the point where we stop reincarnating. We have no more to learn on the physical plane and school is over this time around. We have graduated with honours and will now live for aeons of time in the spiritual worlds.

The Spiritual Worlds

The spiritual worlds constitute the part of the cycle that lies above the two black lines on the symbol. The colour yellow represents the spiritual part of the real human kingdom, as just explained.

The green part, dominated by the energy of intelligence, represents the kingdom of wisdom, where we become the sublime masters of wisdom and where we are the highest capacities of creation of the universe.

The blue part, dominated by the energy of intuition, represents the divine world and here we enter God´s primary consciousness and become one with God. Here we have all answers to all questions and we have access to all knowledge that exists about the universe. It is as high as we can come.

The indigo part, dominated by the energy of memory or bliss, represents the kingdom of bliss or kingdom of memory. In this kingdom we live in our memories of the whole cyclic passage we have completed. It is from the kingdom of memory that all reincarnation into physical matter takes place. Once we have completed the cyclic passage just described and we have lived for eons of time in the spiritual realms, we will again begin to yearn for a contrast to the light and love of the spiritual level. We then begin to prepare for yet another entrance to the physical level. And as before, all manifestation on the physical plane begins in mineral matter. We then enter a new cycle, consisting of the 6 realms, but on a higher level. We have then moved up one rung of the spiral, and this means that we never repeat a cyclic passage.

In all those spiritual realms there is no suffering at all. There we live in bliss, happiness and joy. We occupy ourselves with learning and teaching and everything that is of our interest. It is indeed a very long sojourn in paradise that is awaiting us in the spiritual realms.

In symbol no. 22 Martinus has explained our eternal existence. He has explained what happens after Nirvana, after Paradise, after a life in divine bliss. And thus he has lifted the veil of the meaning of our eternal existence.

As this is a 'nutshell' book, whose aim it is to give the reader an easy and short overview of the arguments for reincarnation, an in-depth explanation of the spiritual realms and of the characteristics of the basic energies lies outside the boundaries of this book. For more expansive explanations of the specifics of these spiritual realms and the basic energies, we recommend you read the book "Death Is an Illusion" by Else Byskov.

Teodicé

The Teodicé concept expresses the problem within theology that aims to explain how we can, at the same time, have a good and loving God and then all the suffering that exists in the world. It is precisely the existence of suffering that makes many people into atheists and godless, because it does not tally with the insisting on part of the religions that a good and loving God exists. But with Martinus' explanation of the principle of contrast and symbol no. 22 it has become clear that suffering is a necessity in an eternal universe. Only the 'unpleasant good' and the 'pleasant good' exist – both are equally important and necessary.

Points to Ponder from Maria:

I reiterate what Else said about printing off the symbols, especially this one because I struggled to follow it until I printed it off and then it was a breeze.

Re: Contrast

Whilst I understood the cycles of reincarnation are for our own soul's learning, and that suffering and pain was necessary for us to develop compassion and thus evolve spiritually, the notion of contrast added a whole new dimension to my worldview. Have you often wondered, as I had, why we can't have happiness everywhere, all the time? When I read Else's book Death Is An Illusion, and encountered the concept of contrast, more light bulbs popped in my head. Of course! If we had no contrast, we would be bored out of our minds and there would be no stimulus for us to experience contrasts. Else's explanation in that book stayed with me – she said that we cannot paint a white picture on a white canvas. I imagined trying to paint a white swan on one and realized that of course, you wouldn't be able to see it. There would be no contrast. In the same way there is polarity. We have to have opposites. It's simple enough when you think about it, but most of the time, we just don't stop to think.

The eternal connection between God and us is the first part of the Symbol that Else explains. Indeed, many people do not believe in God, are atheists or 'hate' God, and all that He stands for. This is largely due to misappropriation of God by mainstream religions. More on this shortly.

God's love for us is eternal. No matter how heinous our crimes, His forgiveness could never be withheld, if we ask for it and truly desire it. The truth is, we are all a part of Him, of his divine creation; we are his children, and therefore He will never reject us. What could this knowledge mean for you in your life now if you are convinced that God doesn't love you, or that he has abandoned you? What if you are racked with guilt over past transgressions or 'sins' that you continue to punish yourself for? Would it not make a huge difference in your life if you could allow yourself to believe that God will forgive you, will never turn away from you, and is always there for you? All you have to do is ask, and it will be given.

Much of our lack of belief or faith in God, for want of a better word, is due to religion. However, as Else points out, God is beyond all religions. It is man who has twisted God's name and used religion in the most warped sense to claim power over people. Historically, kings and queens believed they were chosen by God to rule over the rest of us mere mortals, and they plundered, tortured, killed, went to wars over lands and properties with impunity. The Vatican was equally corrupt and evil, whilst purporting to preach God's word. Hypocrisy in its finest form. Even today, so many wars are waged in the name of God. These are all smokescreens to hide the truth – that religion is mostly about power, corruption and greed. It has very little to do with the reality of who God really is. In light of all this, it is little wonder that so many people have turned from God, falsely believing that He is the cause of so much injustice.

Martinus' explanation of the truth of who God is, is a million miles away from any kind of religious doctrine. It allows us to strip the scales from our eyes and embrace a whole new reality that has nothing to do with religion. The basic tone of the universe is love. That is where our journey is taking us. Back to love and enlightenment. Back to God.

The journey through eternity in Symbol No 22 is clear and easy to follow, and yet it is staggering in both its complexity and its simplicity. What is most amazing of all is the prognosis for the human race, and for the earth – that eventually there will be no more wars, no poverty, and that we will all, each and every one of us, through our lifetimes of suffering and learning, evolve to become man in the image and likeness of God. Complete, compassionate, all-loving beings. Imagine the heaven-on-earth that will come, as Martinus predicts, in 3,000 years.

When you think or feel that the world is a terrible place, that the earth is suffering, that our planet will die, Martinus' work makes you realize that this is not the truth. There is a far greater, more magnificent truth at work and we cannot ever circumvent God's plan.

Re: Teodicé

I have to make one final comment here, and I'm wondering if this concept has jumped out at you like it did for me? How many times have you heard people say, 'There's no God! Or 'How can there be a God if He lets these terrible things happen to innocent people?' I know I've thought it myself, and heard others say it a thousand times. And I've also known many atheists who became so because of this belief that a good and loving God would not allow these things to happen. What a moment of clarity to understand it from Martinus' perspective, and to see the glory in this heretofore unheard of grand design for our life. How can this explanation possibly NOT make sense? Does it not make you realise that there is a reason for everyone's suffering, especially the suffering that seems so terribly unfair and unjust? We have all suffered, and God has seen to it that our suffering is the progression of our souls to ultimately becoming enlightened beings. That may be a very long way off for most of us right now, but there's no doubt in my mind that we will all get there eventually.

8. Conclusion

The one-life theory is still predominant in the Western world. Most people think that we only live once and that the death of the body means that they die, and their consciousness is extinguished. They think they cease to exist when their body expires. This idea is creating a lot of sorrow, anguish, misery, worry, preoccupation and sadness. It means that a lot of people have a totally unfounded fear of dying. The one-life theory is the saddest, maddest and worst theory ever constructed. It sucks. It is a false theory.

The death advocated by the one-life theory does not exist. It is a thought construction that has no foundation in reality. The one-life theory has never been proved. It has never been proved and it never will, because that is not how things are. When we die, we pull our spirit out of the physical body, which was only an instrument. After a rest on the spiritual plane, we reincarnate. We ARE our spirit and I, we are NOT our physical body. Our physical bodies vary as we progress through the cycle as illustrated on symbol no. 22, and death is an illusion. We never die. We cannot die. We can only exchange one physical instrument for a new one. Death is a principle of exchange and renewal. It is not a final destination.

It is great to die. It is a very pleasant experience to pull the spirit out of a body that has been rendered useless through accidents, wear and tear, illnesses or old age. It is like discarding an old, battered vehicle and getting a new one. Death is a divine principle of renewal and for each life we life, our bodies become more and more refined because, as our mentality moves away from egoism and selfishness and becomes more defined by humanitarianism and universal love, our bodies must follow suit. It is the spirit that creates the body as we saw in chapter 5. For each life we live, we become a better, more intelligent, more humane and more beautiful version of ourselves.

This means that our future is bright and wonderful. We shall all become Man in the image and likeness of God – a Man that can only do good and emanate universal love. We are a part of the divine master plan. As it is God´s will that we all eventually become Man in the image and likeness of God what power can prevent it?

Maria's conclusion

In 1966, Elizabeth Kubler Ross's classic, "On Death and Dying", was published, and during her lifetime her books sold millions and were translated into 27 languages. Yet despite the ground-breaking work this gifted doctor and psychiatrist brought to the world, the fear of death still prevails. So why do we still fear death so much? So many of us believe that death is the end, and for those who believe that, of course it seems tragic to lose someone they love but it's even more terrifying to think of our own death. I know many people who believe that there is nothing but oblivion beyond death, that when you die, the lights go out and there is nothing more. This life is it, we only get one shot. So, death is to be feared because it signifies the end of 'us'.

There is also the fear of pain – both physical and emotional. We might wonder if our own physical pain, when our time comes, will be awful and how much will we suffer? Nobody wants to think of themselves being in pain, nor of their loved ones in pain. Then there is the emotional pain. Imagine you are a parent who is terminally ill, and you have young children who need you. Death is the monster that is going to strip you away from your beloved children, leaving them mother or fatherless. Viewed from the one-life perspective, death is indeed a monster to be feared.

And losing a loved one is often (though not always) unbearably painful. We have to go through Kubler Ross's 5 Stages of Grief.

Regardless of whether we believe in life after death or not, we have to go through the loss of their physical presence in our lives, and even when you believe in life after death, you may still have to go through the grieving process. That means tears, sadness, and a period of time to come to acceptance. To not feel these emotions would seem callous, and we are human beings full of human emotion. The loss of a loved one will always be painful to a degree, but I find enormous comfort in the knowledge that our loved ones are just on the other side of the 'veil', in the spiritual realm - the earth's aura. Even though we cannot see them, knowing we will be reunited with them again when our time comes to cross over can bring incredible joy to our hearts. As Elizabeth Kubler Ross ("The Tunnel and The Light") puts it:

'Many people are beginning to be aware that the physical body is only the house, or the temple, or – as we call it – the cocoon, which we inherit for a certain number of months of years, until we make the transition called death. Then, at the time of

death, we shed this cocoon and we are again as free as butterflies, to use the symbolic language that we use when we talk to dying children and their siblings'.

How beautiful it is to think of our loved ones when they have passed over, and ourselves when we do, 'as free as butterflies…'

We hope that you have enjoyed this first 'Nutshell Series' book on the astounding work of Martinus. Else and I have very much enjoyed writing and discussing it during the course of preparing this book. We hope that we have given you enough solid information to decide for yourself whether reincarnation is real or just a fanciful notion. We have provided some of the evidence and arguments that convinced us and we hope that you find the evidence compelling. At the end of the day however, only you can decide for yourself because your journey is yours, and yours alone. May your journey be both blessed and blissful.

A final word: I, Else, can no longer imagine what it would be like to believe that I only lived once. My conviction of my own immortality has crept so much under my skin and my mind has expanded to new dimensions due to my study of the Martinus material, that the predominant world view today with the one-life theory, Armageddon just around the corner, injustice and chance ruling our fates, have become pure misconceptions. I know they are the mainstream narrative and that most people alive adhere to them, but that does not make them the final truth. I am convinced that the final truth lies in the Martinus material. It is huge, and it is logical. There is so much more to the world than what we can see with our physical senses and realizing that spiritual matter is thought matter and that everything arises from thought has made me see that we are alive in a conscious universe. And this universe is God. This is not something I believe, it is something I know.

Biographies of the authors

Else Byskov:

Today I am an authority on the spiritual science Martinus (1890-1981), the Danish philosopher, visionary and mystic and this is my 7th book about aspects of Martinus´ cosmology. But before I came across the Martinus material (comprising over 10,000 pages), I was a convinced atheist for many years, so it came as quite a surprise that I became an author of spiritual books. I was also a searching soul, and because I was looking for answers, these answers eventually came to me. The answers came in the shape of a book about Martinus that ´happened´ to fall into my hands. As soon as I became acquainted with the Martinus material, I got so excited that I had to tell somebody about it, because here I found logical answers to my many questions about life, death and the mystery of both. This resulted in my first book: Death Is an Illusion. A logical explanation based on Martinus´world view. I wrote the book in English and it was published in 2002. You can see all my English books on my website: newspiritualscience.com

Today I am no longer an atheist and I am fully convinced that there is no death: death is an illusion. All my books present the logical basis for this claim.

I am Danish. I have university degrees in Spanish and English philology and I mostly write in English. Four of my books have been published in Danish, one in German ("Der Tod Ist eine Illusion") and the Spanish version of "Death Is an Illusion" was published in 2011 with the title: "La muerte es una ilusión". All my books in all languages can be seen on my website: elsebyskov.com

I also write hiking books. So far three titles have been published in Danish: "Fod på Andalusien" and "Fod på Andalusien 2 and 3". In English I have published "On Foot in Andalucía" which has become an Amazon bestseller. The same book has come out in German with the title: "Zu Fuss in Andalusien". I am an enthusiastic hiker and Andalucía is an Eldorado for hikers with wild, untouched nature galore.

I am a convinced vegetarian (now vegan) and I have written a vegetarian cookbook together with Declan McMahon. The title is: Platefuls of Pleasure and it is also available on Amazon.

I live in southern Spain with my husband. Hiking and writing, as you have probably guessed, are my two biggest passions in life. My children are all grown up.

My websites: www.newspiritualscience.com   www.elsebyskov.com
www.deathisanillusion.dk

On my website newspiritualscience.com you can find all my spiritual books in English and my blog with more than 40 blog-posts answering some of the big questions. There is also a lot of free material to download such as articles, audios, videos, podcasts and free chapters from my books. From the website you can subscribe to my monthly newsletter. Please also see and like my Facebook page: https://www.facebook.com/Newspiritualscience.101/

You can download the first 2 chapters from 5 of my books by clicking on this link: http://newspiritualscience.com/resources/#number6

Maria McMahon:

I was certified in Clinical NLP/Hypnotherapy in London in 1993, and obtained my BSc in Psychology in 1996. Much more recently, (2014) I qualified in Life Coaching and published two books, "Law of Attraction Shortcut Secrets" and "A Pocketful of Thank You", both available on Amazon and other online bookstores.

I'm also fascinated with neuroscience and Brainwave Entrainment, and created "Cogni-Fusion' audio training", a unique type of multi-layered Hypnosis/NLP & Brainwave Entrainment MP3s.

You can find out more at **www.atuneu.com**

I also created "Your Time To Shine", 12 Weeks to Empowered Living, an online coaching programme for women seeking to overcome personal blocks, abuse, and live happier lives.

You can find out more at **www.yourtimetoshinewithmaria.com**
Connect with Me on Facebook
I have several groups and pages on Facebook.
Self-Help, Spirituality & Wellness Books, which currently has over 2,500 members. Authors and readers are all welcome.
You can find out more at:
https://www.facebook.com/groups/selfhelpspiritualbooks
Infinite Self-Worth after Narcissistic Abuse
This is my private Facebook Group for women who are seeking help and advice to overcome Narcissistic Abuse.
You can find out more at:
https://www.facebook.com/groups/infiniteselfworthafternarcissisticabuse/
www.infiniteselfworth.com

And finally you can connect with me directly via my Facebook Business Page:

https://www.facebook.com/infiniteselfworthafternarcissisticabuse/

Apart from my love of spirituality and personal development, I've always loved travel and international culture. Over the last 34 years I've lived in Germany, London, Hong Kong, Dubai, Abu Dhabi and Azerbaijan, and now I live in Southern Spain. I'm an ex-Catholic, animal lover, vegetarian (nearly vegan!) and I share my views of the Mediterranean from my apartment with my three rescue dogs, Levi, Skye, & Reuben. I love connecting with new people and helping to make the world a better place.

I am looking forward to writing more books in the Nutshell with my dear friend, Else Byskov.

Dear Reader...

A final word... if you have enjoyed this book, please take a few minutes to leave a short review on Amazon.com. We are so grateful to you for reading it and would be even more grateful if you would take the time to do that.

Other books by Else Byskov:
"Death Is an Illusion" (Paragon House Publishers, USA 2002)
"Der Tod Ist eine Illusion" (Martinus Verlag, Germany 2006 and BOD, De 2014)
"La Muerte Es Una Ilusión" (Corona Borealis, Spain 2011)
"Døden er en illusion", (BOD, DK 2011)
"The Art of Attraction" (Create Space, USA 2011)*
"Loven for tiltrækning" (Kosmologisk Information, DK 2008 and BOD, DK 2011)
"The Beginning Is Near" (Create Space, USA 2016)
"Ti nye måder at se verden på – På forkant af et nyt verdensbillede" (BOD, DK 2010)
"The Undiscovered Country – A Non-religious Look at Life after Death" (Create Space, USA 2010)
"The Downfall of Marriage" (Create Space, 2016)
"Ægteskabets Nedtur" (BOD, Dk 2010)
"Key Life Lesson from Martinus, the Modern Mystic" (Create Space, USA 2018)
"Platefuls of Pleasure" (vegetarian cook book with Declan McMahon), Create Space 2017
"Glad Mad – en vegetarisk kogebog uden dikkedarer" (BOD, DK 2010)
"Fod på Andalusien – 40 udflugter med indlagt vandring i den sydspanske natur". (BOD, DK 2011)
"On Foot in Andalucía – 40 hiking excursions in Southern Spain" (Create Space, USA, 2014)
"Fod på Andalusien 2 – 25 udflugts- og vandreture øst og nordøst for Málaga" (BOD, DK 2014)
"Fod på Andalusien 3 – 25 udflugts- og vandreture vest og nordvest for Málaga" (BOD, Dk 2016)
"Fod på Andalusien 4 – 27 udflugts- og vandreture vest, nord og øst for Málaga" (BOD, Dk 2019)
"Zu Fuß in Andalusien - 40 Wanderausflüge in Südspanien." (BOD, De 2015)

Other books by Maria McMahon:
"Law of Attraction Shortcut Secrets' (Create Space, USA 2016)*
"A Pocketful of Thank You", (Kindle, USA 2016)

*These two are available as a Book Bundle in Kindle (USA, 2018) https://www.amazon.com/Book-Bundle-Attraction-Shortcut-Secrets-ebook/dp/B072HK4F53/ref=sr_1_1?s=books&ie=UTF8&qid=1545302167&sr=1-1&keywords=Book+bundle+Else+Byskov+Maria+Mcmahon

Bibliography

Books in English:

Alexander, Eben, Dr:
"Proof of Heaven: A Neurosurgeon's Journey into the Afterlife",
Hachette Digital, London, 2012

Bowman, Carol:
"Children's Past Lives. How Past Life Memories Affect Your Child",
Bantam, New York, 1997.
"Return from Heaven", Harper Collins, New York, 2001

Byskov, Else:
"Death Is an Illusion", Paragon House Publishers, St. Paul, USA,
2002
"The Art of Attraction", Create Space (Amazon.com), 2010
"The Undiscovered Country", Create Space (Amazon.com), 2010
"The Beginning Is Near – New Perspectives on Life", Create Space
(Amazon.com), 2016

Haraldsson, Erlendur, PhD and James D. Matlock PhD:
"I saw the Light and Came here". White Crow Books, 2016.

Kübler Ross, Elisabeth, Dr.:
"On Death and Dying" (1969)
"Questions and Answers on Death and Dying" (1974)
"Death: The Final Stage of Growth" (1975)
"To Live Until We Say Goodbye" (1978)
"Living with Death and Dying" (1981)
"The Wheel of Life" (1997)
All published by Touchstone, Simon and Schuster, New York

"The Tunnel and the Light: Essential Insights on Living and Dying,
with A Letter to a Child with Cancer.

Published by De Capo Press, Boston, 1999

"On Life after Death", Celestial Arts, Berkeley California (
1991)

Moody, Raymond, Dr:
"Life after Life" (1977).
"Reflections on Life after Life" (1978), both published by Mockingbird Books, Georgia
"The light beyond". New York, Bantam,1988.

Osis, Karlis PhD & Haraldsson, Erlendur PhD:
"At The Hour of Death", Hastings House, Connecticut 1977.

Radin, Dean PhD.: "The Conscious Universe", Harper Edge, New York 1997.

Stevenson, Dr. Ian:
"Twenty Cases Suggestive of Reincarnation", University Press of Virginia, Charlottesville 1974.
"Where Reincarnation and Biology Intersect", Praeger, Westport, 1997.

Weiss, Brian L. M.D.:
"Many Lives, Many Masters", 1988.
"Through Time into Healing", 1992, both published by Fireside, Simon and Schuster, New York
"Only Love Is Real", Warner Books, New York, 1996.

Books in Danish:

Byskov, Else:
"Døden er en illusion", BOD 2012
"Ti nye måder at se verden på – på forkant af et nyt verdensbillede", BOD 2011
"Loven for tiltrækning", BOD 2010 – alle til salg på www.saxo.com

Martinus:
"Livets Bog" (7 bind) 1932-1960.
"Det evige verdensbillede" (6 bind) 1987-2015.
"Logik" 1987.
"Bisættelse" 1951.
"Artikelsamling 1" 2002.
"Den intellektualiserede kristendom", 2004

Small books:
1 "Menneskehedens skæbne"
2. "Påske"
3. "Hvad er sandhed"
4. "Omkring min missions fødsel"
5. "Den ideelle føde"
6. "Blade af Guds billedbog"
7. "Den længst levende afgud"
8. "Mennesket og verdensbilledet"
9. "Mellem to verdensepoker"
10. "Kosmisk bevidsthed"
11. "Bønnens mysterium"
12. "Vejen til indvielse"
13. "Juleevangeliet"
14. "Bevidsthedens skabelse"
15. "Ud af mørket"
16. "Reinkarnationsprincippet"
17. "Verdensreligion og verdenspolitik"
18. "Livets skæbnespil"
19. "Kosmiske glimt"
20. "Meditation"
21. "Hinsides dødsfrygten"
22. "Livets vej"
23. "De levende væseners udødelighed"
24. "Kulturens skabelse"
25. "Vejen til Paradis"
26. "Djævlebevidsthed og Kristusbevidsthed"
27. "Verdensfredens skabelse"
28. "To slags kærlighed"

Various articles from the monthly magazine "Kosmos", published by the Martinus Institute.

"Samarbejdsstrukturen", Martinus Institut, København 1992.
"Gennem dødens port – søvnen og døden" (hæfte).
"Vejen til den sande lykke" (hæfte).

All booklets, Kosmos, and articles have been published by Martinus Institute, Mariendalsvej 94-96, 2000 Frederiksberg, Copenhagen, Denmark.

The website of the Martinus Institute is: www.martinus.dk – parts of Martinus´ work can be read online in English from the website.

Made in the USA
Middletown, DE
12 August 2019